MENGHEDI

3/15/14

To: Tures

Many blessings on your journey!

Menghedi

Two Women.
Two Journeys.
One Hope for Freedom.

Semhar Gebre

HALPIN
PUBLISHING

Published by Halpin Publishing
ISBN-13: 978-0-615-93354-2
First Printing

Halpin Publishing
1976 S. La Cienega Blvd., #440
Los Angeles, CA 90034

For Mom, Dad, Sewit, and Alai
For my superman
For Eritrea

ACKNOWLEDGEMENTS

I would like to humbly acknowledge my wonderful and hard-working parents, Gebrehiwot and Weyni, who fled from a war-torn Eritrea and immigrated to the United States in the early 80s. Raising children as immigrant parents, I later learned, was the hardest job they had ever faced. I have always been deeply moved by their dedication to their children's lives and education. They pushed forward, even when they were in a country where they could not understand the language and were treated poorly for it. Their unconditional support and continual guidance has shaped me into the woman I am today. Without them, I would be a lost soul.

I wish to honor my sister and brother, Sewit and Alai, for their patience, unconditional love, and sense of humor at times when it was most needed. I would also like to thank my sister for the title brainstorming session for this book. While I offered *Yellow Brick Road*, which she still teases me about, Sewit came up with the beautiful title, *Menghedi*. This title, one meant to inspire others while on their journeys, has meant more to me than she will ever know.

I would like to extend my profound gratitude to my *Proverbs 31* man for his love, patience, and undying faith in me, even when, at times, I lost these within myself. I am indebted to him for his words of encouragement and inspiration when I felt like tossing my drafts into the Pacific. "Just remember, in some space and time, your book is already done," he would say. This journey would not have been the same had it not been for my soulmate and the love of my life.

I would like to thank Lull Mengesha of Lull Mengesha Publishing for the LMP Publishing Scholarship for First-Time Authors. I am grateful for Lull's guidance with the publishing process and his sound advice.

I wish to acknowledge my editor, Erin McCabe, whose tireless efforts pushed me to think differently and taught me how to breathe life into my characters. Erin's hard work and dedication to the field are traits I wholeheartedly admire and I am grateful for the working relationship we had on this project. I would also like to thank Amanda Brown for her editing services and insightful thoughts.

I gratefully acknowledge G. S. Prendergast for the cover artwork.

For being the best writing partner and encouraging me to take leaps when faced with project challenges, I would like to acknowledge my good friend, Semhar Debessai. I am incredibly grateful for her words of advice and the impeccable timing at which they have come.

I would also like to thank the countless family members and friends who sent well wishes throughout my journey with this novel. From phone calls to e-mails to social media messages, their outpouring of love and positive energy uplifted and inspired me to be the best possible writer I could be.

Each of you have contributed to my *menghedi*, or journey, and I will forever be grateful.

"For I know the plans I have for you," declares the LORD, "plans to prosper you and not to harm you, plans to give you hope and a future."

Jeremiah 29:11

PROLOGUE

Hide nothing, for time,
which sees all and hears all, exposes all.
—Sophocles

Cloaked in the coal-colored pious garb of a Muslim wife, she hurried alongside a trail of torched homes. Her disguise was cunning, melding her frame perfectly with the darkness of the night. In the past week of wearying travel throughout Eritrea, it was her camouflage at dawn among devout civilians on their way to morning prayer. She pressed her veil tightly across her face, shielding her identity from the world. Every move she made was one of purpose. No one was to recognize her face. No one was to discover her name.

Quicker, she thought, *push harder.*

The bare, sullied soles of her feet struck the ground swiftly. Time was of the essence. The courier in the village of Unah, identifiable by the red fabric sewn on her sack, lived by one rule—a missed appointment meant a missed opportunity. They were to meet at the center of the largest and most eventful marketplace by daybreak. But if delayed, she risked the departure of the courier and would retain the message seated in the heart of her hand with little hope of another chance for delivery. A missed appointment with the courier would have made for a dreadful ending to a grueling expedition—five days and nights of pounding the grounds throughout the villages of Turmuz, Ishukh, and Hamid, covering nearly 200 kilometers. She shook her head vigorously. Failure was simply not an option. She would be on time, even if it meant each blister on her heels and between her toes was ripped apart by the hardened twigs and shrapnel that met nearly every step she took.

You aren't walking fast enough, she scolded her feet.

She shifted her eyes from the ground into the distance, skillfully keeping her pace. Beyond the towering leafless trees, she searched for signs of civilization—lanterns with life, smoke from the roofs of panicked families, military vehicles belonging to the Ethiopian regime—anything to suggest she actually *was* close.

A faint light emitted from the west. It may have been the spark of a fire set by the regime or an Eritrean informant relaying a safety signal to absconders, but the reason for the sign was of least importance. She was approaching Unah, and the flicker of light was all that was needed to ignite hope within.

She hastened her pace, just shy of running, her heart racing faster than she. The four corners of the folded letter dug deeper into the calluses of her palm, but pain was no stranger. It had become a companion on this lonesome journey, reminding her she was still alive.

"Guide me,
push me,
on my
way.
I'll

pro-
tect
you,
and I
beg
of
you
the same."

She sang in whispers, distantly surveying every ravaged home she passed for activity. The Ethiopian regime was infamous for pouncing on the unsuspecting. She synchronized her words with her footsteps. It somehow blurred her focus on the hours remaining. She leapt at the anticipation, wildly building as she repeatedly envisioned the moment of surrendering the letter. Her breath began to shorten, but she continued to sing. It forced her to steady her breathing, and more importantly, it kept her sane.

"*Guide me,*
push me,
on my
way.
I'll
pro-
tect
you,
and I
beg
of
you
the same.

Guide me,
push me,
on my
way.
I'll
pro-
tect
you,
and I—"

The air intensified in thickness within a matter of minutes, and the stillness which once offered freedom to move about rapidly vanished. She slowed her pace and moved along stealthily. A once thriving village had been reduced to remnants and ash. Homes lay in ruins, belongings incinerated beyond recognition. She rubbed the tip of her nose aggressively. The stench of decaying bodies and burned homes was growing increasingly overpowering and required more attention than her lullaby. A typical scent throughout her childhood, it was revisiting, haunting the path to Unah.

She halted in her tracks and stood deathly still. To her right, the human remains of charred civilians lay scattered among the devastation. Beside a withered bush, there lay the foot of a child, dismembered from the rest of its body. She forced her occupied hand to her stomach and the other over her veiled mouth, gasping for air that suddenly seemed scarce. When the tears stung, she exhaled in whimpering puffs, sinking in stance with each breath. Nausea triggered from the depths of her womb, and her tears transformed the bodiless child into a blur as she wept, thinking of her own.

"*I'll protect you, and I beg of you the same,*" she sang as she caressed her swollen belly and packed love in the words meant for her child.

"Why aren't you here?" she whispered to the skies. "How could you leave me to do this on my own? I long for you more than I do our child's arrival. How could you forsake me?"

She tapped her forehead, the middle of her chest, and each shoulder before she mouthed a prayer for the soul of her child's father and the victims sprawled on the road. She even sent a request for redemption on behalf of those who caused hell and Earth to collide —those belonging to the Ethiopian regime.

"...forgive them, and as you would forgive them, I ask forgiveness for myself."

Hatred for the Ethiopian regime was rampant, and even though she prayed in their favor, she once shared the same intensity as her fellow Eritreans. The regime was responsible for years of terror on the innocent, while Eritrean separatists battled on the fields to free their nation. She lived in a time where the ringing of rifle shots, the booming drums of grenades, and explosions of land were a part of daily living. They were a people drenched in fear, much like the benzene that poured over their homes as they helplessly witnessed their children burning alive.

She pinched her nose and inhaled deeply through her mouth, turning to the lights of Unah.

Forward. Keep forward.

***

Two hours passed and she was upon the village of Unah. She arrived within range of the marketplace and was minutes from meeting the courier for the first time. She perspired beneath her guise, her palms saturated with nervousness. She searched the sea of white and black garb for a flash of blood red fabric patched onto a sack. Men and women compelled by religious fervor shoved past her, chanting verses to themselves as they briskly walked along the dirt roads. They gravitated toward the morning duty of prayer, drawn by the amplified voices blaring from small speakers at the highest points of the church and the adjacent mosque, respectively preaching the word of God and Allah. The worshippers were obedient in their uniformity of dress, wearing their religious identities on their backs and draped around their heads. They even etched their faith onto their skin as it was common to see the sign of the holy cross permanently inked on the foreheads of devout women.

She stood there, immobile. The stretching pain that lingered for the past hour was becoming unbearable. Several minutes elapsed before a brand new feeling consumed her—panic. It heightened with movement. Each footstep forward was one of apprehension and meticulousness, and despite the cautious placement of each heel, the electrifying sensation refused to cease from bolting through each shuddering limb. The unborn child threatened arrival with far too little time to prepare. Civilians, laborers, and the pious continued to swarm the roads contributing to the usual commotion of a Sunday morning, and yet, not a single soul noted her labor.

My tongue! Why isn't it working? Have I gone invisible to these people? she thought.

She placed trembling fingers to her mouth under the garb, protruding her tongue between her lips. It was dry and seemed twice its normal size. Control was gradually slipping further away. She spun around in place multiple times, hoping to attract the gaze of an onlooker, and still, she remained unnoticed.

Someone, please pay me mind. Anyone!
Am I going to bear this child here in this market?
Right here on this patch of dirt?
Lord, is this the fate I deserve?

She searched for answers to make the quaking cease, but it was internal and unrelenting. The imminent perils facing her and her child weighed heavy like a set of bricks on the crest of her head, pressuring her to crumble. Limbs were not supposed to feel like liquid. She grew weary, energy rapidly escaping through her toes and fingertips, stinging her skin upon exit. In a matter of seconds, she collapsed to her knees. Forced to the heels of her palms, the writhing pain and pressure from her womb were too severe to remain upright. Surrounding her wounded body, between the multi-colored stone wall of the church ten or so meters to her left and the marketplace straight ahead, talks of faith and produce coalesced in the air. And yet, not a single breath was exhaled in her favor.

She shifted her weight and turned toward the wall of the church. While the panic diminished, delirium took its place. Countless mouths emerged from the wall, pleading for monetary mercy. She closed her eyes and kept them tightly shut for seconds before she opened them again and viewed the same image. Only this time, the mouths were floating. A string of hallucinations overshadowed her reasoning.

A wall of moving lips.
Moving lips!
How will they see me with no eyes?
Have they been punished, too?

Levitating hands gripping onto collection cups replaced each set of lips, and bewilderment soon followed.

Hands?
Lord, give them eyes!
I need them to have eyes!

She crawled on her knees in the direction of the mystical wall, balancing herself on all fours. This was a journey of its own. She released her right palm from its grasp on the pebbled dirt road and with it pressed upward beneath her navel. It was the only way to persuade the child for more time. As she drew closer to the wall, the supernatural mouths and hands transformed into frayed-clothed panhandlers.

Identical to a bump in the road, travelers found their way around her without batting a compassionate eye. Mule drivers, farmers, and the devout alike made no expression to suggest they had even seen her. Still, despite the lack of empathy among them, she kept forward. Someone would have to take notice—someone who understood what it felt like to plead from the ground.

Pay me mind.
Forget them!
Forget your tin cups!
Just look my way, please.
Lord, make them look my way.

The din coming from the collection cups grew louder. Only a few meters away from the church wall, her tongue regained its sensation. She rolled the muscle in a native dialect and repeatedly begged for their supporting hands.

"Please, help me. I'm with child!" she exclaimed.

The path between herself and the beggars cleared of travelers for a short time as she locked eyes with each of the six women crouched against the church wall. They rose from the ground slowly, the holes in their muddy brown rags exposing their emaciated bodies.

One dropped her collection cup in disbelief, while two dove for the fallen coins and scurried off jeering. The women looked around them and soon formed a huddle around her, a group of four, enclosing the scene with their bodies. They no longer examined her. Instead, they peered into each other's eyes, saliva running down their mouths, and hunger reeking on their breath.

"Hurry, look to see how much she has."

"Drag her over there, behind the stand. Pretend you're helping."

"Here, put this in her mouth."

Speech escaped her once again as she watched a dirty handkerchief dangle in the air above her head.

"No, you fool! Put that away. Let her cry. It'll look like she's gone into labor."

The exchange of each word pricked her heart like the sharp edge of a butcher knife. Her anguish, though, was the least of their concern. Roughly handled and clamped in their arms, they let her slip onto the ground behind a bread stand. She crashed onto her side, her head thumping against the ground in the fall. She brought her knees as close to her stomach as her child would allow and embraced herself with all of her might. Death never smelled so real.

My own sisters? How could you betray me? she thought.

She stared into a sea of footsteps belonging to a people who strolled the market in normalcy. Letting go seemed simple when no one cared to even pay attention to the robbery. She had no strength left. The beggars turned thieves searched her long garb for pockets and coins. She responded with her hands above her head in submission. The end was near, her spirit broken by the death of her love and the betrayal of friends molesting her body for their next meal. Surrendering seemed like the only thing left to do.

Between their feet and the large spaces of the stand, she caught sight of the color red on the back of the courier moving farther away. The symbol on the sack she carried was just as her friend had described, a patch of fabric dipped in goat's blood, and it was leaving the marketplace. She outstretched her arms, and still clutching onto the letter, she wailed.

"No!"

She ripped apart the bottom of her disguise, exposed and weeping over the *missed opportunity*. She watched their faces as they began to recognize hers. One by one, the mouth of each beggar dropped. A gasp broke the silence.

"It can't be…how did she get here?"

"*What* is she doing here? How is this even possible?"

"Good Lord! Is that—"

"*Shhhh*, hurry, cover her face!"

The women rushed to shield her. The patrols would soon emerge in teams with their weapons propped on their shoulders. She cried, no longer for the physical pain, nor for the company of the betrayers her long lost childhood friends had become. Instead, she wept for her fate, and more so, the courier for adhering to such a foolish rule.

The stretching pain occurred yet again, and when it did, she released a howl far louder than the goat being slaughtered in the nearby meat market. Once it subsided, she managed to speak again.

"Get someone, please," she begged once more for her life.

The old friends lifted her gently and placed her against the church wall. They dispersed into the crowd still remaining within earshot.

She watched from the ground, doubled over in pain. The beggar who had threatened silencing her, waved her filthy cloth in the air at a number of uniformed doctors and nurses who rushed in for their workday less than a kilometer away. Of more than fifty medical workers, only one cared to offer an ear to the typical racket of the panhandlers—a young nurse wearing a mud-spattered uniform, much like the dirt on the beggars' rags.

"Please help! Not for us," the beggar yelled, pointing to the church wall. "It's for her."

"Who is she?" the nurse asked as she accompanied the beggar.

"She's—"

"We don't know!" blurted another.

"Are you alright?" the nurse asked as she approached.

She offered the help who had arrived no answer.

Wasting little time, the nurse ran back onto the busy road, now swarming with mules and goats. She grabbed a market worker's arm, nearly toppling his empty wheelbarrow.

"No, I can't. The patrols…," the market worker hissed as he approached. He looked to the entrances of the church and mosque as if he were in hiding. His words were loud enough to dash her hope.

"Will *this* change your mind?" The thinnest of the beggars waved a coin from her cup in the air, and within seconds, the worker agreed.

Consciousness was slowly escaping her body as the party of six placed her into the transport. The nurse seized her hand and ran alongside the barrow.

"Not to worry, we're rather close," the nurse shared.

She clenched the nurse's hand in response.

"My name is Almaz. What is your name, dear?"

But the rock-strewn path bumped her back against the barrow, the agony rendering her speechless. After several minutes, the jarring road no longer fazed her. She was slipping away, her awareness fading. Blackened circles formed in her periphery until they collided and expanded. Her eyes remained ajar, and yet, the world had become pitch black. Without her permission, her thoughts were leaving.

This was never supposed to happen. Not to me…

CHAPTER 1

Three things cannot be long hidden:
the sun, the moon, and the truth.
—Buddha

Hearsay spread like scorching flames naturally would in the blazing heat. The mysterious woman in labor at the marketplace in the village of Unah captivated many tongues. Details surrounding the morning events, reaped by a farmer whose land neighbored the hospital in which the childbearing woman screamed for God's mercy, were planted in the anxious ears of an eavesdropping schoolchild. The nine-year-old girl prematurely thieved the narrative on her lunch break, just as two classmates had robbed her only meal of the day. Using her hunger-driven imagination, she recited *her* version to a street sweeper, who cleaned the jumbled words to make for a credible drama. A local one-eyed goat herder caned all the facts from the story and, in telling his wife about his day's work, offered a thrilling depiction of a woman who awakened four times from the dead before departing—and, there was still a chance she would resurrect again.

But it was Almaz, the nurse responsible for rescuing the pregnant woman from the center of the market, who had stitched the truth of the matter to her own heart. It was a story she had vowed to never reveal in its entirety, and yet, her circle of friends were on their way for more answers and their daily dose of gossip serum —coffee. Kept scathing hot, the aroma of morning *boon* was infamous for keeping women awake and alert for hours as they sipped along to hair-raising stories shared in secrecy, stolen from the streets of Eritrea.

Almaz slumped in her uniform, exhausted from the buzz surrounding the mystery woman. She sat in the courtyard of her uncle's home, the home of the one-eyed goat herder, and together with her uncle's wife, they awaited the arrival of the remaining circle of sisters.

"Almaz…I warned him not to tell those lies," her uncle's wife began.

Almaz folded her hands in her lap, crossed her ankles one over the other, and tucked them underneath her chair. "Uncle *cannot* continue to spread lies about that woman, and I," Almaz continued, pressing her forefinger's nail deeper into the center of her chest, "*cannot* have my name attached to this."

The wife of the goat herder nodded her head in agreement. She pressed her forehead as far into the web of her hand as it would go and sank deeper into her chair. She confided, "Your uncle's just not the same." She tapped both temples with her index fingers and pinched her eyebrows together.

Almaz agreed, "They are dirty bastards. He walks around with a hole where his eye should be, and they go about their days as if life is grand."

"Their hands…the hands of the Ethiopian regime are merciless," said her uncle's wife, examining her own palms.

Almaz sympathized. After her uncle's confrontation with the

regime one year prior, his mental stability had deteriorated, and his storytelling had become far too perilous to ignore.

"He *has* to be more careful. That is exactly how he ended up this way—having discussions with random people with no regard for the truth. What if they overhear him talking about her? Do you want them here questioning him again? Do you want them here questioning *me* for helping her? And if they find I had anything to do with this...so help me God, I could be *killed*. You *know* that."

"My Almaz, leave your uncle to me. I'll make it my duty to make sure he keeps his lips sealed. In the last decade of marriage I've been successful in getting through to him. In the meantime, you have to start believing you did what was right for that poor girl. Just imagine what would have happened had no one taken notice of her at the marketplace. Both she *and* her child would have died."

"At least I would have never known about it." Almaz brought a stinging thought to words.

"Nonsense. There is no room for regret in this house," her uncle's wife admonished.

"You don't understand." Almaz released her ankles, sat her elbows on her knees, cupping her face in her hands. The frightening cries and the gory images began to play again, forcing her to bury her face in her hands. The woman's body, dressed in placenta and fluid on the metal table in the center of the hospital room, lay lifeless, while Almaz consoled a hollering motherless newborn in her arms.

"What is it that you are hiding? What is haunting you? Tell me," her uncle's wife pled. "If you tell me the entire story, I can help you work through this fear. Open up to me," she persisted. "Open up to *us*. When the sisters arrive, you'll have an entire tribe listening to you. Think of how that will change what you are feeling. Be strong, Almaz."

Almaz kept her face buried. She agreed, "I'll release it when we're all together." There was no trust like the trust of the sisters. They were a coterie of twelve women, including Almaz and her uncle's wife, who were forever bound by their covert gatherings of coffee sipping and healing.

"Good. I urge you to keep faith," her uncle's wife consoled.

Almaz raised her head from her hands at the sound of tapping on the side window of the house.

"Do you hear that? Right on time…for you. There is a reason you heard their knocks right after I told you to keep faith. Do not lose sight of that." Her uncle's wife smiled and wagged her finger in the air. She believed everything was a sign from above.

Almaz watched from her chair in the center of the courtyard as her uncle's wife hurried toward the side entrance to their home and opened the small door. The tribe of women, all ten, scurried into the bedroom. The regime's soldiers at the end of the road were on patrol duty, and the women avoided the front door for this reason. Any signs of gatherings provoked interrogations. Her uncle's wife kissed each of the women thrice on alternating cheeks and signaled them to enter the courtyard where Almaz sat surrounded by a circle of eleven empty chairs.

"How did you rest? Did everyone sleep well?" her uncle's wife greeted them all.

"Praise be to God, we are fine. We are good, glory be to God," a few of the women responded. Their voices harmonized with the flock of birds chirping in unison overhead, creating a melody of hellos. The others had quickly found seating next to Almaz, who rocked in her chair, detangling her hair in one moment and rubbing her arms with her hands for warmth in the next.

"Come, have a seat." Her uncle's wife ushered the rest to the un-occupied chairs.

Almaz's cousin appeared from out of another bedroom to help her mother. The child skipped to the kitchenette to prepare sweetened bread and pastries on a large tin tray for the guests. She made her rounds to each woman, lowering the platter before them, offering a small meal to accompany the miniature cups of *boon*.

"May we be so fortunate as to see your wedding." Each woman repeated the ultimate blessing in response to the child's discipline —that the child would soon be endowed with the honor of a husband. It was the greatest blessing a young girl could receive, transforming from her father's daughter to her husband's wife. Almaz's cousin bowed her head in timid receipt of the words from each of the elders and replied softly, "Thank you."

Her uncle's wife rose from her stool and approached the tribe of women with a small pot of coffee beans she had been roasting while her daughter served. She held onto the elongated handle of the pot and shook its contents to infuse the air with more of its scent. The women waved their hands in the direction of their noses for the aroma to come closer. They repeated, "Very good, exceptionally good."

"May the goodness be returned in your favor," she replied and bowed her head at the expected praise.

Why can't I be that collected? Almaz thought.

Almaz sat upright in her seat, staring into space. Everyone in the room continued about the morning routine as though the news to be shared was light. She knew what they were thinking—coffee was a cure. It had always possessed this power of healing. The tribe would talk and Almaz would share everything with them, and all of her memories would vanish into the air along with the coffee vapors. She knew her tribe of friends and their patterns of thinking all too well. Only this time, there was something *they* did not know about *her*. Almaz tapped her feet, loudly but unintentionally. She knew she could not tell them *everything*.

Her uncle's wife began to grind the coffee beans with the assistance of a headless hammer. She placed the coffee grounds into the *jebena*, a ceramic coffee pot with a heavy, round base, a lengthy neck, and a short spout stuffed with the hair of a mule as a filter. At the boiling point of the *boon*, and with no small talk left to share, her uncle's wife broke the awkward silence, leaving instead a welcomed hush over the room. She leaned over and whispered, "Almaz has something she would like to tell us."

Almaz looked up from her lap. Her head traveled the room and found eleven sets of eyes peering at her.

She cleared her throat before beginning. "It was me. I was the one who helped her to the hospital," Almaz admitted.

The farthest seated from Almaz across the circle, the wife of the disfigured road builder spoke in a low tone and asked, "Did the child survive?"

Almaz knew they had come prepared with questions and looking for answers to the holes in the stories they had been hearing from her uncle.

"Please, let me start from the beginning," Almaz replied. Recollecting was difficult as it were, but she promised for her own sake that she would retell as much of the honest accounts of that Sunday morning as she could, from beginning to end.

"We put her in a barrow," Almaz recalled the urgency, "before the patrols began their day."

"Who is we?" asked the wife of the maimed welder, ignoring Almaz's first plea.

"Myself and a market worker with an empty barrow. I found it odd, though. She was being cared for by street dwellers, the ones right outside of the church."

"Really?" the wives of the wheelchair-confined schoolteacher and the facially-scarred shop worker, two sisters with few gray hairs apart in age, asked in unison.

"I've never seen a street dweller give up her money to assist anyone," Almaz continued, raising her hand in the air still in disbelief. "One of them actually *paid* the man with the barrow to help the woman get to the hospital. I figured they must have witnessed something that made them pity her, but there was no time to ask. I had to get her to the hospital."

"Was she a beggar herself?" asked the wife of the deafened spice vendor. "What I mean is, why would she be with *them*?"

"No, she wasn't *with* them," Almaz replied, trying to keep her composure. "I never got the chance to ask her how she got there." Almaz twirled her hair. The first lie was born.

"Did you find the beggars afterwards and ask them who she was?" Almaz listened to the wife of the maimed welder as she dug for more.

"No, I haven't seen them since. I've looked for them, but they've disappeared from the church," Almaz remained intrigued as she spoke, "and no one I ask knows of their whereabouts."

"How could they simply vanish? Those women have lived on that road for at least five years," the spice vendor's wife wondered aloud, frowning.

"Who was the woman? Where did she come from?" the wife of the toothless butcher chimed in for the first time.

"Is her husband a freedom fighter? Is that why she was running away?" the sisters added to the series of questions.

"Wait, she was running away *from* here?" The wife of the disfigured road builder paused. "Impossible. We would know who she was," she concluded.

"Please, allow her to finish," her uncle's wife spoke against the interruptions.

Almaz listened to every question left unanswered. They were legitimate ones, questions she would have asked had she been in their seats. She paused.

"I don't know." Another lie seamlessly rolled from Almaz's tongue. It brought a churning to her stomach. "We rushed into the hospital," she continued still attempting to satisfy a morsel of their curiosity, "and the man from the market tried to assist me in putting her onto a table. The other nurses saw us struggling and ran to help." Almaz fixated her eyes onto her lap again, not wanting to see the faces of her sisters.

They would never understand why I risked my life for her, why I was willing to be hung for a stranger. They aren't meant to know, she thought.

"I held her hand until we reached a room, and as soon as we transferred her over to a larger table, I went to go light a candle in the corner. She slipped out of consciousness again, and I felt responsible. I thought it was because I let go of her hand to light the candle." Almaz felt the words rushing from her mouth. She stopped for a moment to regain her breath.

After a moment's rest, Almaz persisted with her one-sided conversation. "She was still breathing, though. Her eyes were closed, but she was still alive. There were seven of us nurses in that tiny room, and the doctor hadn't even arrived yet. Why there were seven of us, I still don't know. A few of them wanted to see who she was and sought answers for why a woman dressed as a Muslim was heard screaming for Jesus and Mother Mary from the entrance of the hospital. When she *was* able to speak, she refused to give her name. It soon dawned on us that she was in hiding and fearful of being captured, but the *why* was still a mystery."

Forgive me Lord, Almaz prayed in between her woven lies. *I'm no better than my uncle.*

Still, she continued, "We all felt she had a story, but given her condition, she wasn't exactly in the right frame of mind to tell it. Six hours of labor—that is how long our hope had us fooled into thinking she would live."

Almaz lifted her chin. She faced her tribe of sisters. "It felt like death was an uninvited guest that had shamelessly barged in at the peak of her labor, and it was diverting all of our attention, causing more chaos than the day would have preferred to entertain. If the air in that room had touched *your* tongues, it would have tasted much like castor oil, promising for a wretched aftertaste and a series of skipped heartbeats." Almaz patted her chest rapidly, simulating the frenzy of her heart in the hospital room.

The anticipation was building for everyone, including the wife of the disfigured road builder. "Did the child live, my Almaz? Did she make it?" she persisted.

"She lived," Almaz replied. "She lived. She came out kicking and thrashing her arms." Almaz demonstrated, smiling at the memory. "It was the sign of life for which we had all been anxiously awaiting, holding our breath until the first cry echoed throughout the room. But the birth of that beautiful little creature came at a steep price." Almaz held her heart in sorrow for the motherless newborn. "The child took her first few breaths of life at the very same moment her mother took her last. The final thrust that woman made was the same stroke of power that tore her life away," Almaz explained. "At the same time, we could hear the pitter-patter of the regime just outside. We could not mourn, so together, we pressed our hands over our mouths to keep our cries from being heard." The comprehension spread across the courtyard. Mourning the loss of an Eritrean life during these times and on this soil was punishable by a torturous death.

Almaz absorbed the silent reactions around her. Faces contorted, frowns filled the room, and some wiped their tears with their *netsella*, the traditional scarf of an Eritrean woman. The telling of unsettling stories did not usually evoke responses such as these from the sisters and, during a moment of silence, Almaz identified the reason for the change. She was certain that her sisters, all of whom had children of their own, were not shedding tears for the news of another lost life, but for the mystery woman with no identity—the woman without a known mother or father to inform that their daughter was no longer breathing.

"We wept for the child's mother and equally so for that hero of a child," Almaz proclaimed. "I cradled her in my arms. One of the nurses pushed the door of the room open for a little light as the one in our room had extinguished. The other nurses formed a soothing huddle as I carried the child in the center. Even with the commotion that surrounded us, with warplanes thundering above, how ironic that a newborn would have what we so desperately desired—serenity, in all of its glory. In her first few minutes of life, she had a far more fascinating story than any of us."

Almaz stood from her seat, wiped her tears, and embraced each of her tribal sisters, offering them kisses goodbye. "I am going to be late for work," she explained. She held her uncle's wife a little longer than the rest. The wives were clearly disappointed by her early departure, but she assured them, "We'll talk again tomorrow."

Almaz stepped out from the same side door through which her tribe of sisters entered and shut it closed behind her. She exhaled deeply, relieved to be liberated from the eyes and ears of attention. She checked for patrols both ways, and when the roads seemed clear, she reached for the letter scraping her chest beneath her uniform. There were parts of the woman's story she swore she would reveal to only one person. She kissed the letter and vowed again as she had to the woman before she departed.

"Your daughter Ma'arinet will carry her name of Equality with pride. Trust that she *will* know your story."

CHAPTER 2

I dream of giving birth to a child who will ask,
'Mother, what was war?'
—Eve Merriam

"Miriam, are you ready?" Timneet shouted from her own front step toward her best friend's house only two doors down. She flicked the buzzing fly that landed on her wrinkled, army green school uniform—sewn by her mother, it was longer than the other girls', one that danced about her ankles as she walked to school every morning, protecting her from the regime's desire of little girls and their legs.

"Hallo!" Timneet yelled again from her own doorstep, turning toward her friend's door. She expected a lanky Miriam to sprint and meet her the way she had every morning since the age of six. Instead, Timneet's ears met silence.

"How are you *always* late?" Timneet mumbled, her eyebrows collapsing in confusion. She stopped biting alongside the nail folds of her middle fingernail to suck the blood that was now trickling.

It was a Saturday morning, the last school day of the week, and although she ran the risk of being tardy for class by waiting for

Miriam, Timneet would not dream of leaving her best friend behind. *Always travel in pairs,* Timneet heard her late mother, Rosa, warn. The regime preyed on the lonesome like a pack of salivating hyenas searching for their next meal, cackling mid-drip.

Come on…open. Timneet brought her arms to her side like a soldier, clenched her fists, and locked her gaze on Miriam's front door. She leaned forward as though preparing to rocket like a missile, practicing what she and Miriam swore they would someday achieve—moving objects and people about as they pleased, not to mention parting the Earth.

One day, I'll break the ground and throw them all to hell. Miriam's words rung loudly in Timneet's head like a cowbell, disrupting her concentration on the door. Hell was the one place Miriam spoke of often after the regime tied a group of nine screaming women together and threw them into a roaring fire pit. The group of women included Miriam's mother, Aster.

And after you do that, I promise I'll break the sky and bring both of them by our sides. They'll never have to leave again. Timneet's own voice boomed in her head. She called to memory her own mother sitting in a pool of blood in the middle of their courtyard. As quickly as the thoughts flooded her mind, Timneet rushed them back out. She squeezed her eyelids shut and shook the image from her head.

"We have to get to school," she muttered.

Timneet turned to the paint-chipped black door of their meddlesome neighbor, the home of Aregeet, and the only barrier between Timneet and Miriam's doorsteps. Aregeet was an old toothless woman, half-Ethiopian and wholeheartedly denying her Eritrean side by secretly working with the Ethiopian regime as a spy, at least, according to Timneet's grandmother. Vicious as she was, Aregeet's lies about Timneet's family led to many midnight raids in their home and because of this, Timneet's grandmother made her vow to never look into the old woman's beady, spell-casting eyes.

Be careful, child, Timneet could hear her grandmother caution, *because Aregeet has the power to make you tell the regime your name is Zewdi, just so she can accuse you of telling a tale.*

Timneet's grandmother also made her promise to never walk past Aregeet's door of death. So, she leapt instead.

Traitor, Timneet mouthed with her hand as straight as a spear on the side of her face, shielding her sight from Aregeet's door.

"Miriam," she called more softly so as to not awaken Aregeet's curiosity. Seconds passed and the silence grew louder. Timneet tapped her fingers on her lap and bounced her legs as she snuck peeks behind her shield of a hand at Aregeet's door.

Miriam's front door, propped open with a manure-stained stone the size of Timneet's head, allowed anyone who passed by a glimpse of the family's washboard, full clotheslines, and several pots and pans scattered on the ground. Timneet poked through the opening and swayed her head in search of Miriam's face between the flapping sheets. Miriam's father and brother, Abo Ande and Samson, sat with empty plates on a crooked table as Miriam scrambled by and placed food on their dishes. It smelled like buttered bread and *berbere*, the spice that made Timneet's mouth water even when her stomach was fully satisfied.

"I'm sorry." Miriam rushed to the door, struggling to find the shoulder strap of her book bag for her flailing arm.

"Why don't you wake up earlier?" Timneet asked as Miriam shoved Timneet backward and shut the door behind her. And, just as quick as Timneet's reaction was to scold, she followed her question with regret and said, "I'm sorry."

You should be more understanding, Timneet reprimanded herself.

Since her mother's death, Timneet watched Miriam transform into the woman of the household, attempting to keep afloat in school while cooking, cleaning, and fetching fresh water for her motherless family.

"Where's Amaniel?" Miriam switched the topic as they traveled up the hill, taking the longer route to school. They would soon make a left and on the next street, Via Beccini, another left. They landed on Via Vialetti and made a right, finally in the correct direction for school. Avoiding Aregeet was worth the extra ten minute walk.

"He's still sick. He's staying home again."

"That's four days of missing school. Your brother is so lucky!" Miriam exclaimed.

"He's also behind in his studies. He's not going to be lucky when he gets back to school next week," Timneet answered, giggling.

Timneet took hold of Miriam's hand in her own. The Ethiopian patrols were heavy in number this morning. The number of rapes and murders at the hands of the regime had risen drastically in the past few weeks. This also meant that the number of schoolchildren who would risk their lives to escape and join the liberation effort was climbing.

"Did you hear about Rusom?" Timneet asked, twisting her mouth to face Miriam on her right while looking directly ahead, keeping watch for the patrols and any sudden movements. *There really isn't a point to keeping watch,* Timneet reasoned. There was absolutely nothing she could do or say to protect herself had a gun suddenly whipped her face, sending her body from this village to the next. Despite this thought, Timneet continued to scan the crowd.

"No? Do you have news?" Miriam asked with the same stretch of her cheeks and curve of her lips.

Their entire seventh grade class was shocked to learn of Rusom's disappearance the week before. The boy, who kept them all laughing despite the thunder of the planes capable of releasing explosives at any given moment, had run away to join the freedom effort for

Eritrea.

"He won't be helping in the struggle anymore." *It is the best way I can put it,* Timneet thought.

"Did they catch him?" Miriam's voice wavered.

Maybe this is not the best time to share. If Miriam suddenly started wailing, Timneet feared the patrols would not waste a minute before tying them to the same fate as Rusom. "I'll tell you when we get to school."

"No, tell me now," Miriam demanded.

"Promise me you won't change your face?" Timneet asked, still surveying the crowd for any patrols who looked like trouble, usually the ones leaving the bars this early in the morning.

"I promise," Miriam said.

"They found him. Amaniel said they hung him from a tree some place here in Zigib."

"Dear God!"

Timneet continued, "Amaniel said that the regime is saying two runaways from our school are two runaways too many." Their other classmate, the smartest of them all, a boy named Abiel, hung from a pole outside of a meat market only a few weeks prior, his legs skinned. "We have to be careful. They are threatening anyone who uses 'free' and 'Eritrea' in the same speech."

Miriam halted abruptly, jerking Timneet backward. Timneet followed Miriam's gaze to the sight ahead across the dirt road. Flies swarmed a decaying body just outside of a bar playing the songs of Tilahun, the legendary Ethiopian singer, from a yellow music box.

"I can't stand it anymore…," Tilahun bellowed.

Timneet yanked Miriam's hand forward and leaned into Miriam as they walked, unintentionally pushing her until Miriam's opposite shoulder brushed against the doors of houses and a few strangers.

Neither can I! Timneet yelled within, thinking of the singer's words.

A few meters ahead, Miriam's nails dug into the surface of Timneet's hand. Timneet raised her eyes from the ground. Two bodies hung from the same tree. The last time Timneet stared at dangling corpses, nightmares ruined her sleep for months. She protected her dreams the same way she avoided Aregeet, with a hand for a shield between death and her eyes.

Timneet wrestled with the right words to speak, but silence seemed more appropriate than anything else.

Three patrols emerged from another bar, striking their clubs on their palms. They stared, causing Timneet's heart to alternate between stopping for seconds and racing crazily. She hastened her movements, forcing Miriam to keep up with frequent tugs.

Lord, please let us make it to school safely, she thought.

***

"Good morning children," the straight-backed Ethiopian soldier stood at the front gate entrance of Timneet's school and greeted each child with a cigarette threatening to fall from his lips as he spoke. The wide doors leading to the courtyard were fully open, exposing the other five soldiers as they waited gripping their wrists with their hands.

"What is it?" Timneet whispered, concerned with the smiles planted on the soldiers' faces.

"I haven't a clue," Miriam answered, shifting her weight onto the balls of her feet to see over the taller children in front of them and past the gates.

Together they waited in line to be checked off the regime's list. Timneet listened to her hopeful schoolmates behind her.

"I've never seen such faces."

"They almost look like they're happy."

"And…with us," another added.

"This can only mean one thing." There was glee in the boy's voice. "Our prayers have finally been answered!"

"Thank you Lord, thank you Lord. You see, Timneet, you see, Miriam," their good friend Lula shared behind them, turning them toward her with a firm grip on their shoulders. "I told you there would be a day." Timneet laughed as Lula squirmed with excitement, squeezing her younger brother Tedros' hand. She lifted his arm, beaming. "We are the champions," Lula whispered.

Tedros, half the size of his older sister, giggled.

Another friend, Alem, whispered, "This is the beginning, my friends. There will be a day when *they*," she carefully pointed to the soldiers with her arm close to her side, "won't even be here."

Henok, a good friend and classmate of Timneet's brother Amaniel, smiled. "Something *is* coming. I can feel it," he said.

Timneet and Miriam turned to each other. Timneet could interpret the look on her best friend's face. It was one of uncertainty, and Timneet felt the same. After all, since when had they ever placed their trust in the regime?

"Good morning, thank you for your service."

Timneet received a nod and a surprisingly gentle pat on the head from the soldier to whom she recited her name. Five more times the girls repeated the phrase, once to each soldier as they bowed their heads and made their way into the school quarters. The atmosphere beyond the gate entrance was alive. No one had ever seen the regime conduct themselves as human beings.

"Line up in your queues," Memhir Petros, Timneet's teacher ordered the students. The soldiers closed the gates after the last entry, a young boy named Zaccarias who wobbled toward the queue for grade four.

As they had done every morning, grades one through eight stood in straight lines from the left of the schoolyard to the right in ascending order. All but one soldier had moved from the gate en-

trance, planting their feet before Timneet and her schoolmates—
two pairs stood on each end of the yard, and one soldier swayed in
the center, still holding onto the list of names, while the gate guard
stayed in the back with the teachers of the school.

"Amaniel Melke!" he yelled the name of a child who had not yet
reported for school, barking at the queue for grade eight where
Amaniel should have been.

Timneet watched her fidgety friends as they all turned their
necks in her direction. Her older brother Amaniel was ill, home
with a high fever and deathly chills after running into mosquitoes
near the river one week earlier. The soldiers knew this and they
still called his name in such a way that suggested he was a runaway
like the others.

"Amaniel Melke!" the same soldier exploded again. He muttered
a few words to the soldier on his left, folded the piece of paper in
half, and tossed him the list of names. The receiving soldier scribbled a minute's worth of notes onto the sheet of paper before placing it on the floor.

"Today we have something very special for you. But first, let us
hear the anthem!" The middle soldier, the most decorated of them
all, wore a number of different colored ribbons on the top of his
beret. He spoke with the deepest of voices, deeper than Timneet
had ever heard from a man, and loud was his only volume. His
voice boomed as he talked, and although Timneet was not one of
them, among the lines were schoolmates who closed their eyes as
he spoke.

"One, two, three," the soldier roared.

Timneet watched the girls and boys in the courtyard sing excitedly, raising their fists to the skies as they shouted the nation's name
through forced smiles and clapped with each syllable thereafter.

"Ethiopia land of our fathers
The land where our God wants to be
Like bees to a hive swiftly gather
God's children are gathered to thee.
With our red, gold, and green floating for us
And our Emperor to shield us from wrong..."

Timneet moved her lips but she would not dare give *their* song her voice. Instead her heart sang a tune of her own, one for Eritrea.

Eritrea, Eritrea,
They may have us sing their name
But we have you in our hearts always.
There will be a day when these streets will be yours
And the whole world will know your song.
God bless your people and your beloved name...

"*...the greatest nation of them all.*" When Timneet's schoolmates finished, she watched the looks of satisfaction take over the soldiers' faces.

"We're going to play a little game today," the decorated one announced, puffing his chest out like a regal bird, "one I guarantee you have never played. Girls, sit down right where you are, and boys, line up against the back wall over there." He continued to instruct, "Line up according to your grade level, and hurry!" The gentle smiles the soldiers wore at the front entrance vanished and the barking of the regime returned.

Lula leaned in closer to Miriam who sat directly behind Timneet at the front of the seventh grade line, whispering to them both, "Did they plan a surprise show with the boys? Why didn't Tedros tell me about this?"

Timneet shrugged, not wanting to seem too concerned.

Tedros stood with his back against the wall as told, to the left of the older boys.

Timneet read the utter confusion on the faces of the boys, and a sinking feeling took control of her body. She looked at Miriam behind her and saw she had shut her eyes tightly.

Miriam feels the same way I do. Something is wrong.

Timneet and the other schoolgirls looked at one another and the range in emotion expressed on their faces seemed to go from joy on the left side of the yard to confusion and suspicion where she sat on the right.

The next few minutes rocketed at a speed which no one could equate to time.

"Boys! Step your backs as close to the wall behind you as possible. Face us and your schoolmates, you rats," roared the decorated one.

Whimpers met Timneet's ears from the back of her queue. She turned around cautiously. Lula had buried her head in her hands, shaking it from side to side. Her legs remained folded like Timneet and the other schoolgirls, only her feet which were locked beneath the backs of her thighs dug deeper into the ground as she swayed back and forth.

Timneet turned her attention to the boys again. With a clear view from her front seat, she observed their attempt at conversing as they looked at each other for answers.

Tedros put his palms forward facing the sky, twisting his wrists in what seemed like uncertainty. Markos, the boy beside him, shrugged his shoulders in response.

"Is everyone ready to play the game?" the soldier yelled.

With a rapid wave from the decorated one's hand, the soldiers removed their weapons hanging from their backs and cradled them in their hands. The decorated one marched from Tedros' end of the line to the other where the oldest boy in the school, Henok, shook in his sandals. The smile and hope he displayed while at the gate entrance minutes before entering the school quarters had been ripped from his face.

Whimpers swiftly turned to cries—the ones Timneet heard often on the walk home through Zigib when patrols were inside of homes. Timneet understood, and by the sounds coming from her schoolmates, they did too. Torture and death were nearby.

"Quiet in the yard!" the decorated one bellowed.

As he paced, the decorated one began with a speech that sounded as though it had been rehearsed for some time. "When I was a child, almost your age," he pointed to Tedros, the youngest of the group, "I listened." He ran his fingers through the lengthy hairs on his chin. "There were no alternatives to being a well-behaved child, and lacking the discipline to listen to my elders was worthy of a beating." He stopped in place and played with the corners of his mustache.

"Abiel Gebreyesus and Rusom Mehari. Do these names sound familiar to any of you?" the soldier asked, calling out the names of the two runaways, their former schoolmates, whose shared fate was death by hanging.

"You see children, punishing Abiel and Rusom was not a good enough lesson," the soldier went on to explain. "When Abiel was punished, the message was lost because Rusom ran out and did the very same thing. If the lesson had been learned, Rusom would have never thought it was an idea worth risking the same consequence. Am I correct?"

The crowd of girls had cried enough tears to fill a river, including Timneet who wept for more than the trouble that met her friends —her tears included ones of gratitude for Amaniel's absence this morning.

Amaniel needs to run! Timneet's thoughts were frantic. Her family had seen far too much bloodshed within the corners of their small home in just one year's time. *I must get home and warn him!*

"I asked a question!" the soldier barked.

"Yes," Timneet mumbled along with the rest of her schoolmates.

The soldier of highest rank continued, "If you don't like the game we play today, you'll never have to join the fun again, but it is your choice. You are the determining factor of whether this game will ever be played from this day forward. It all depends on today's lesson," he bowed as he spoke the key word of the day, "obedience."

"You on the end there," the decorated one pointed to Tedros, "announce your full name."

Jittery and hunched over, frightened by the two armed soldiers standing less than a meter away, he muttered his name, "Tedros Yemane."

"Louder!" The officer raised his fist, flexing his muscle. Timneet watched helplessly as Tedros nearly jumped out of his own skin.

"Tedros," the boy yelled, proclaiming his name, looking over at the decorated one who continued to march behind the backs of the other two soldiers.

"Do you have any brothers or sisters, Tedros?" He stopped, facing the crowd of girls as he barked.

"I have one sister...Lula." Tedros pointed behind Timneet and Miriam. Lula quavered in her seat.

"Lula. And tell me Tedros, what are the names of your parents?"

"My father is Yemane and my mother is...Yodit," he uttered. Tedros cried as he finished speaking his mother's name.

"I promise this will be the last question, Tedros."

The little boy nodded, sneaking a peek at his sister, seeming relieved that the game was nearly over.

"How old are you?" the soldier snarled.

The little boy put up three meek fingers on one hand and three straighter fingers on the other and spoke the number to the soldier,

"Six."

No sooner than Tedros could finish speaking the numbers on his fingers, six shots rang in the air. Three bullets spewed from each of the weapons held by the two soldiers standing nearby and met Tedros' defenseless body. The screams heard from the young girls across the yard and the rest of the boys along the wall were unlike any sound Timneet had ever heard. Lula fell to the ground, convulsing. Timneet and Miriam quickly crawled to their friend's side.

"Girls, do not touch her!" the officer boomed. "It would be best if she went to be with her brother, the *natural* way. Unless, of course, you both want to leave us the way Tedros has," he growled.

Timneet and Miriam scrambled back to their places, sitting closer to one another than before.

Timneet caught a glimpse of their teacher, Memhir Petros, at the back of the schoolyard along with the other teachers behind the queues. Some stood with their shoulders hiked, others with their hands on either side of their heads, and the remaining two teachers covered their mouths with both hands stifling what surely would have been cries. The soldier nearest the gate entrance rushed to them as Timneet watched their eyes follow what she imagined to be Tedros' body slumping to the floor. Only she didn't have the stomach to face the wall again and see if it were so.

"On the ground, all of you!" the soldier ordered the teachers, waving his gun.

Save them! Save us! Timneet wanted to yell at Memhir Petros. Fearing the sight of holes in Memhir Petros, Timneet returned her eyes to the wall.

"And you," the decorated soldier continued as Tedros' body bled next to the child at which he was pointing, "your full name." The second boy in the queue, Markos, seven years of age, clung for dear life to his eight-year-old brother Abraham by his right side.

"Separate yourselves immediately!" the soldier ordered, his voice cracking with anger. When the brothers failed to obey, the two soldiers responsible for Tedros' murder approached them, ripped their tiny hands apart, and threw them onto the floor beside one another forward from the line of boys along the wall.

"What are your names?" the commanding soldier asked.

The brothers were unable to answer any questions. Timneet watched as they both opened their mouths, but no sounds were heard.

"You see girls, this only proves the earlier point I made on obedience in this school and how you *all* are clearly not understanding," the decorated soldier said, starting another rant.

The brothers looked into each other's eyes. With a nod from Abraham, they bowed their heads and recited a prayer.

"Our Father, who art in heaven,
Hallowed be thy name
Thy kingdom come
Thy will be done…"

The soldiers looked at one another, enraged. "Stop this at once!" they snarled.

Timneet looked to the boys' sisters in the crowd, Freweyni and Azeb, in the queues for grades five and six. They were mouthing the same words as their brothers.

"…as we forgive those who trespass against us." The sisters seemed to gain power through the words, making themselves heard as they chimed in with their brothers from their seats.

"What do you think you're doing?" the decorated soldier asked the boys. By the time the children reached the end of the prayer, they were back in each other's arms, facing a crowd of jaw-dropped schoolchildren, including Timneet.

"You two, both of you, face the walls." Markos and Abraham rose from the floor and turned their backs to their sisters and the rest of the crowd. They refused to disengage from one another. Markos hunched over and wrapped his arms around his older brother's waist, nestling his head into his brother's chest. Abraham grabbed hold of his younger brother, interlocking his fingers around Markos' shoulder.

"Ten!" the decorated soldier exclaimed.

Ten bullets from one gun and ten from another met the backs of the brothers. Their bodies sank to the blood-stained floor, still in full embrace, now spiritless.

"Children, do you see what happens when you disobey? When you don't answer our questions? We answer for you!" the decorated one shouted, pointing to Timneet and the girls while the soldiers behind him laughed until tears filled their eyes. The shots continued to ring. Shots of nine, ten, twelve, rang loudly through the air as they met the flesh of innocence. More than a dozen bodies lay in pools of blood.

"Don't you have any children, sir? Have mercy on us!" Henok pled for his life to be spared. "Think of your children." Henok dropped to his knees and whimpered, "Please."

Without the skip of a beat, and what seemed like not an ounce of remorse, the soldiers fired their weapons. Timneet flinched fourteen times as the booming shots rang through the air, one by one, striking Henok repeatedly in the chest and head.

Tears rolled down Timneet's face. She sat in her seat, paralyzed. This was the regime. This was their *game.*

The lead soldier turned to the only children left in the school—the girls. "You are dismissed. No class for the rest of the day."

The decorated one walked over to the teachers and warned, "If you touch those bodies, you'll have the same done to each and every one of you." He pointed at the teachers still crouched on the floor along the wall opposite the massacre.

As they made their exit, Timneet heard the soldier who had been in charge of the teachers, amuse his comrades with a joke as he shuffled his feet. "Did you hear the one about the camel and the fisherman?"

The soldiers cackled as they left the school quarters with the blood of Timneet's schoolmates and friends trailing behind their footsteps.

***

Timneet and Miriam sprinted home. The wind was on their side.

"I have to tell Amaniel to leave!" Timneet exclaimed.

"Timneet, be careful. Aregeet may be on her morning walk."

"Amaniel and I long planned for this day, Miri. We have a secret code," Timneet whispered as they slowed down at the sight of patrols. "I have to tell him he should go get some coffee dipped in spice."

"What an odd code. Who would dip *boon* in *berbere*?"

"No one, that's why it's a code."

They arrived at Timneet's home where the front door was left ajar.

"Adey?" Timneet called for her grandmother. She pushed the heavy door with both hands, peeking around it. There were no soldiers present.

Adey sat on her favorite stool and laundered clothes in the wash basin with the swiftness of a seventy-year-old woman.

I still have time to warn him, Timneet thought. "Hello, Adey." She darted past her grandmother, leaving Miriam behind at the front door.

"Your friend has no manners," Timneet heard her grandmother tell Miriam.

Timneet barged into their shared bedroom hoping to find Amaniel snuggled underneath the bed quilt where he had rested throughout his illness. She found an empty cot with its sheets on the floor instead.

"Her brother at least hugs me when he sees or leaves me…so tight. You know he almost broke my ribs today doing just that?"

"Adey? What did you say?" Timneet darted back into the courtyard, panting. "Where is Amaniel, Adey?"

The old woman continued to hum.

"Adey," Timneet repeated as she dragged her feet to Miriam at the door and faced her grandmother. "Where is Aman?" she asked, moving her lips slowly for Adey to comprehend. There were times when Adey's ability to hear was worse than others.

"Oh," Adey replied, "he left minutes ago. I'm surprised you two didn't see him. You could've asked him to bring you something back from the market."

"Amaniel went to the market?" Timneet asked.

Standing side by side, Miriam pressed her palm harder onto Timneet's shoulder in a side embrace while both of their eyes grew wider than the Red Sea.

"Yes, it was the oddest thing, my child. I thought he would want to get some medicine for himself, but he said he would bring you back *boon* dipped in *berbere*." Timneet's grandmother guffawed as she rose from her seat and pinned clothes to the wire overhead. "Whoever heard of such a thing?"

Timneet lowered her head, her knees buckling.

Before a drop to the ground could make a sound loud enough to alarm Adey, Miriam swiftly turned to face Timneet and caught her fall with a tight embrace and a lift from the ground. "Be strong for her, Timneet," Miriam whispered in her ear. "Stand up," she said more firmly.

Timneet planted her feet to the ground again, but the hurt was still suffocating, making it nearly impossible to speak.

I'll never see him again. Here I am rushing to get home, hoping to give him one last kiss. I should be grateful he left in time, but why then do I feel like I've been knocked to the floor? Timneet faced her grandmother as Miriam's hand returned to uphold her outside shoulder. *It's just me and you now, Adey. I pray you don't leave me, too,* Timneet silently wished.

Adey hummed Amaniel's favorite tune as she hung his school shirt.

"I should make that boy a new uniform, *mish*? Tell me if I'm wrong Timneet. Does this shirt look too small for your brother?"

***

Do it, she thought, *be a man.*

While fighter planes threatened to plunge missiles atop the heads of least suspecting civilians, Timneet was preoccupied with a more targeted assault in her own home the very next morning. She stared down the barrel of an assault weapon and in her thirteen years of life, confrontations such as these had come to be much too habitual for her liking. Four soldiers of the regime stood in her front yard with their neatly pressed tan uniforms and colorful berets. Two soldiers stood near the tall metal framed doorway, on guard, while the remaining pair interrogated Timneet.

"Where is your rat of a brother?" The trigger finger of a dark-lipped, stout, village terror—a soldier of the regime—shook vigorously, his veins protruding from his forehead as he spoke.

"He *isn't* here," she replied, sternly. "I already told you."

She fought the urge to blink—she didn't want to miss seeing the bullet that possessed the power to end her childhood. Timneet longed for the shots like she yearned for the lives of her two sisters after they had been struck by bullets. She desired the holes in her body like she craved her father's warm embrace after his arms had been amputated by the regime's multiple machete strikes. She wished for the speedy sounds of life ending like she prayed for her mother's resurrection after being raped, not once but on six separate occasions, left to die in a pool of blood after the last. She longed to be with her precious family once again, even if it meant she would have to feel the pain they felt in order to get there.

"Well, it looks like we have a tough one here." His calmer partner and leader of the pack, a giant compared to his companions, chuckled. "Let me advise you of one thing," he said as he leaned forward. "You have a painful day ahead of you if you don't cooperate, little girl." The patrol rubbed the back of his hand alongside Timneet's cheek and moved onto toying with her hair.

His touch sent countless bumps to her skin.

"Sit!" the stout one ordered, sending Timneet to her knees with a thrust to the top of her shoulders.

She met the floor abruptly, her dress collecting dirt while there. The regime's patrols had flung the plant-filled benzene canisters that once decorated the corners of the small courtyard. She caught the smirks and ugly pride of the two guards with their noses high in the air as she was forced to face them at the doorway.

"Hands behind your head," the stout patrol continued shouting orders, flapping his large lips wildly.

Timneet interlocked her fingers behind a stiff neck and patiently awaited the bullet that would remove any trace of misery. She prayed it would come swiftly and reunite her with the peace that came when she was in the presence of her mother, father, and sweet sisters. At the hands of such cowards, though, it seemed like they weren't ready to kill her just yet.

The bastards are here to torture, Timneet thought.

"We can *see* he isn't here, you little scum. Where did he go?" The stout patrol stepped forward, still aiming his weapon.

Timneet kept her eyes wide open and faced his weapon with the resilience and bravery that escaped not only children her age but most men just the same. The massacre had erected a shell around her heart.

"What is it that you want from us?" Timneet asked.

"Answer the question and there is no harm," the leader of the pack reasoned. He bent his knees near her side and went on. "You don't answer my friend's question," he pointed beside him at the shaking gun, "and we have a problem. Do you like problems, little girl?" he asked as he tugged at her ponytail. "Because we hear your brother seems to love problems."

The two guards left their post, joining their partners.

The stout patrol pressed the end of the weapon forcibly between Timneet's eyebrows, pushing her head backwards past her heels and forcing her to topple onto her side. Timneet turned onto her back as the patrols closed in, unbuckling their belts.

They're going to attack me like they did mama. They're going to make me scream! Timneet's hardened heart melted with fear. She was a child again, no longer wishing for a bullet, but for a chance to run instead.

"Timneet. Timneet, who was it at the door?" asked her grandmother, only now managing to move from the back of the house to answer the angry knocks from earlier.

The men stopped, startled by the sound of company. Timneet had tried to act as though she were alone. The last thing she wanted was to involve her ailing grandmother.

Timneet!" Adey's trembling voice continued calling behind her.

Her heart plunged as the footsteps of the old woman came forth. Timneet lifted her neck and rotated toward the entrance to their guest room where her grandmother stood gripping the door's frame for balance. A chronically round back bowed Adey's head to the floor, so that she had eyes for nothing but the concrete under her wearisome feet.

The stout patrol sharply shifted Timneet's gaze with the end of the gun's barrel guiding her cheek back toward him and his colleagues, towering over her body. He rocked the weaponry like a pendulum between her eyes, threatening to rob yet another life from their home.

"Adey," Timneet whispered for her grandmother so as not to cause alarm. When Timneet's call went unanswered, the soldier closest to her, one of the two who had kept guard, motioned with the waving of his rifle for Timneet to call her grandmother again. "Adey, please," Timneet turned again, softly speaking.

Her grandmother uttered no words to suggest she had heard Timneet's calls. The patrol jabbed the end of the barrel into Timneet's cheek while another used his rifle near her throat and lifted her chin, forcing an upside down view of Adey. Timneet erupted with an agonizing cry. Her grandmother lifted her head and hurried her eyes to Timneet lying on the floor. The old woman grew pale, latching onto the side of the door.

"Oh, Lord! I beg of you, she has nothing to give you. She has nothing you want," Adey pled with the soldiers, her voice tired. She was a woman still in mourning, wailing secretly into the night behind shut doors, as the regime hung those who shed tears over the loss of Eritrean life.

"Please, please, don't touch her. You took my husband, my children, my children's children," wept the old woman, crumpling to the floor. "Don't take my little one, please. She's all I have."

Timneet understood where her anguish came from. The elderly woman's wailing broke Timneet's thoughts. She listened to her grandmother cry for mercy. The language of compassion was one Timneet knew the patrols deemed incomprehensible as their faces seemed to be painted with strokes of confusion whenever they heard such cries.

Adey nestled her face into her wrinkled hands and sobbed in an

43

all too familiar scene. Her grandmother's hoarse cries emitted from exhausted lungs, drained from years of torment.

"We're here for Amaniel," said their leader. He motioned the others toward the kitchen.

Timneet knew what they entered kitchens for, and their intentions were filthy. She remained on the floor, propped up by her hands offering Adey consoling looks.

"If no one seems to know where he is, then you suffer," barked the stout patrol.

Timneet watched as the soldiers pulled out cooking spices and flour from the kitchen and emptied out the contents onto the floor between Timneet and Adey. The patrols mixed all the contents with their feet. It was their way of ensuring that finding their next meal would be difficult and that they would remember *them* for it. As horrible as it was, the act suggested that they preferred them to suffer—but suffering also meant they would let them live.

"We don't know where he is," Timneet replied as her grandmother wept for their food and the constant struggle that seemed to be an everlasting curse in their home.

"She's telling you the truth," her grandmother validated Timneet's statement, breathing heavily with each word.

"He was sick, and then we don't know where he went," Timneet continued.

Ignoring the cries of the old woman, both the leader and the stout patrol focused their attention on Timneet. "On your knees! Hands at your neck!" the stout soldier snarled.

Timneet obeyed, moving cautiously.

"I'm going to ask you again and I'm warning you, little girl," the leader spoke as he approached Timneet, "this is your last chance. Now, tell me. Where is Amaniel?"

Timneet found herself in the way of their operation, halting a momentum that instilled fear across the village of Zigib. Thoughts raced through her mind while she stared down the barrel of the gun again. *Is this really it? Is this the way my time ends?*

"Are you certain you don't want to tell me where that rat is? He *happened* to be missing from school yesterday when we extinguished all the other rats?"

I guess we're blessed…sometimes, she thought.

From the vertex of her head to the balls of her feet, a warm sensation took hold of her body, as urine trickled down the inside of her legs, still bent at the knees.

Damn you for making me embarrass myself! she cursed the soldiers. This would surely be seen by the soldiers as a sign of weakness, and although she was unable to control her bladder, Timneet refused to have them see her in such a childlike moment. "I do not know," Timneet whispered. She squeezed her seat, pressing further into her heels, so as to stop the flow and keep from being ridiculed or worse, targeted for torture. The regime had a longing for preying on the helpless, most especially those who were visibly meek or afraid. Timneet silently prayed that they would either kill her or leave. To see her weak would be a death all on its own.

"Stand up, little girl," the leader of the pack commanded.

Just as Timneet convinced herself to ask for her life to be taken instead, a chilling scream came from what sounded like a man down the road.

"Help me! Someone, help!"

A second later, the voice cried, "Why are you doing this to me?"

The soldiers flung their heads to the entryway, and Timneet struggled to recall the man behind the voice. He sounded familiar.

The stout patrol grabbed the other's arm. "We must investigate. It is likely that dirty group punishing the rascals at the Old Italia courtyard again."

"Again? Why are they in Zigib? Do they not care that this is *our* territory?" barked one of the guards.

"I've warned them plenty of times that we would handle the people here," shouted their leader, seeming astonished that another group of patrolmen would take their jobs.

"Stop, my legs! Help!" yelled the voice again.

Who is that? Where have I heard that voice before? Her heart raced.

The stout patrol lowered his weapon and balled his fist. "I'll show them."

I hope the man runs away before you catch him. Why does another have to suffer for me to live? Sadness met her lips and pulled them into a frown. Ultimately, it was the possibility of there being another body to torture, to maim, an opportunity to destroy the peace of mind of another human being and an entire family.

As the soldiers rushed to address the screams, one pointed to Timneet just before leaving. "We're not finished here."

I hope you all trip on your own feet and bump your heads on rocks! she thought to yell.

When the front door slammed behind them, Timneet's grandmother threw her head scarf to the ground and rubbed her old knees as she sat next to the ruined spices and flour. She chanted to God, every spirit, saint, angel, and every prophet. *"Amlakh, Yesus, Adey Mariam, Mikiel, Aregawi…,"* Adey sang.

Even still, Timneet's belief remained—they would be back with their machetes and guns, with their violating hands and breath reeking of the infamous *areqi* liquor.

Timneet rose from her seat rather slowly, her knees aching from kneeling for the past hour. She attempted to walk toward Adey, but something was terribly wrong.

Timneet looked behind her at her seat.

This isn't urine! she squealed inside.

A small pool of blood lay on the floor. Timneet patted her body in search of holes, beginning with her face, down to her chest, and continuing until she ended at her feet.

"Is it possible that I could have missed bullets striking my body? How could I have not heard or felt such a thing?" Timneet wondered, speaking gently so as not to alarm Adey.

She ran her hands over her feet wildly, looking for the slightest of wounds. As she continued toward her head, feeling her legs, belly, chest, searching for areas she may have overlooked, drops of blood fell from between her legs. Wide-eyed, Timneet placed both hands on her chest, one atop another and remained still in horror with only one bone-chilling thought racing through her young mind.

Not only can they pierce your soul, they can make it bleed, too!

***

"Good morning, Timneet," Miriam's brother Samson announced from his seat across from his father. Miriam had removed the sheets and clothes hanging from the line, and the view of the breakfast table was clearer than before. It was almost as if Samson and Abo Ande had not moved in the two days since Timneet was last at their doorstep.

"Hi, Samson," Timneet replied from the doorway with her eyes to the ground, kicking pebbles as she waited for Miriam. Although Aregeet had departed for the bus station to Keren where she visited her sister every Monday morning, Timneet's nerves were not entirely convinced.

Timneet looked up again, not wanting to seem impolite. "Good morning, Abo Ande."

Miriam's father gave her a nod in return.

"Are you doing alright?" Samson asked, twirling his empty plate on the table.

Miriam must have told him Amaniel ran away, she thought. "I'm fine, thank you. And you?"

"Listen, about yester—," Samson began.

Miriam barged into the open kitchen, nearly throwing Samson's bread on his dish. "We have to go, Samson," she interrupted, widening her eyes and pointing at their father with her head twice. "We can talk later." She gave her father his meal and kissed him goodbye, gently. He barely moved at the sweet gesture, his eyes never leaving his late wife's shawl wrapped around his neck. With no father of her own to kiss, Timneet fought back tears.

Miriam dashed to the door and whispered her usual morning greeting, "I'm sorry."

Timneet embraced her closest friend for a long time, venting—the ordeal of the previous day calling for an extended hug.

Miriam grabbed her sack at the doorstep and took hold of Timneet's hand, leading the way off the rocky pathway and onto level ground. They walked quietly until the patrols were no longer in sight. Miriam broke the silence first when they reached the foot of the hill, making a right toward school.

"Did you hear Samson yesterday?" Miriam asked.

"Hear Samson? When? Where?" Timneet kept her eyes on the road ahead, bracing for patrols to emerge from the corner stores or the bars as they continued to speak with twisted lips.

"*Yesterday?*" Miriam emphasized.

"What do you mean?" Timneet had too emotional of a day to remember any interaction with anyone other than the soldiers in her family courtyard. She stopped tapping the side of her thigh and thought, *I didn't even see Samson yesterday.*

"Help, help," Miriam whimpered. "What does that remind you of?" she asked through a smothered mouth, waiting for a reaction.

"What are you talk—?" Timneet rested her words.

"Help," Miriam continued to jog her memory, only quieter this time.

I won't believe it until she says it. I have to hear it from her first, Timneet thought.

"Please, help," Miriam continued.

"It was *Samson*...and *you*?" Timneet released her hand from Miriam's grip and placed it on her face. "Are you mocking Samson?" she asked bewildered as they continued their walk, almost forgetting the emotionless face pact she entered with Miriam for the sake of deflecting any attention from themselves.

Miriam only nodded in response.

"You're the reason I'm still alive? You and Samson? Why?" Overcome with emotion, Timneet searched her friend's face for an answer, her throat swelling. Her eyes filled with tears, stinging with the sensation to keep them from causing streams down her face. She turned to her best friend and embraced her again with all of her might.

Miriam defended her act with Samson. "They call us rats? They're the true rats."

"You shouldn't have done that. You both could have been killed if they had known," Timneet stressed.

"You could've been, too. Besides, it was Samson's idea. Now, stop squeezing me. You're too much." Miriam had never been the sensitive type.

Timneet attempted to untangle herself, but her long locks intertwined with Miriam's necklace. Soon, they were caught in a hysterical laugh that neither could shake.

"I hate your necklace," Timneet whined in the middle of giggling, forgetting her fear of the patrols. It tugged on her hair, and was more painful than when her grandmother braided it. Miriam's necklace was an intricate piece of jewelry that hung so beautifully around her neck, a silver chain with a dark blue pendant in the shape of a dove. Aster had given the necklace to Miriam, and since her mother's murder she guarded it with her life. There was not a single day Timneet could call to memory when Miriam did not have her necklace on. It was the only connection Miriam had to her mother and it made Timneet wish she had one of her own.

"There you go." Miriam untangled the last few strands of Timneet's hair and brushed her clothes off. Timneet had wrinkled Miriam's uniform during her display of affection.

"Thank you, Miri. I can't believe you saved me. Thank you, thank you."

"Timneet, stop it already. And, stop crying. I know you would have done the very same," Miriam explained.

When the girls arrived across the street from the school, the grip shared between their hands tightened. Timneet felt the sweat drip from the nape of her neck down her back. Miriam proceeded forward, only Timneet yanked her hand back.

"I'm not ready to go in yet."

"I know, but we must," Miriam explained firmly.

"Miri, what if they kill me because they can't find Amaniel? Or worse, what if today is the girls' turn? What if they kill us all? You can't tell me you haven't worried the same since Saturday."

"Nonsense, Timneet. They target the boys…not us."

"But, we're *girls*, Miri. They can do a lot worse than kill us." Timneet forced her exposed toe through her sandal and into the dirt. She kicked the road as though the soldiers were on the ground, stalling their entrance into the school. *Don't you remember what happened to my mother?* Timneet thought to ask.

"No, we will be fine. Now hurry before we're beaten for missing," Miriam warned.

I don't want to! Timneet rebelled inside but obediently followed Miriam instead.

The girls rushed across the dirt road.

"Names!" The lead soldier ordered the girls.

"Miriam Weldekristos," muttered her best friend.

Timneet hesitated before obliging to his roar and instead envisioned a machete magically appearing in her hands, using it to cut him in half at his waist. She was quickly awakened by a hard nudge from Miriam and a bewildered look that shouted, *After everything Samson and I did for you?*

"Your name!" the lead soldier hollered again while reaching for his club, seeming annoyed that he was having to ask her more than once.

Her eyes darted from Miriam's pleading eyes to his cold, villainous face and back again to Miriam. "Timneet Melke," she replied while still looking at her closest friend.

The girls were shoved through the entryway where they were met with a stinging stench. Swarms of flies found a new home on the cold skin of the dead. They held their noses and mouths, and because there were no soldiers in direct sight, Timneet and Miriam stepped closer to the heap of corpses belonging to the boys who were once their friends. Twenty-eight lifeless bodies were piled atop one another within the school quarters. The instructors were ordered to neither remove nor fiddle with the flesh to whom the soldiers gave the term, *would-be troublemakers.* More sickening than this was the command directed to the families of the children —they were not to collect their sons nor bury their remains until seven days had elapsed.

A little girl struggled to lift the weighty bell and bring it back down without striking her knees, calling for the schoolgirls to hurry and get in their queues. The girls were pushed to line up in the courtyard a short distance from the rotting bodies. It was time to sing the national anthem.

"Ethiopia land of our fathers,
The land where our God wants to be
Like bees to a hive swiftly gather
God's children are gathered to thee..."

The soldiers heckled throughout the entire song.

"Clap harder for your leaders…for your country!"

"Jump. I'm warning you, jump higher."

"Where are your smiles, you rats?"

With guns aimed at their heads, the girls jumped their knees to the skies. The anthem came to a close and the soldiers departed, leaving the girls to scatter to their classrooms. Timneet and Miriam held hands instead and crept closer to their friends.

Timneet leaned to her right where Miriam stood, and without taking her eyes off the bodies and the flies that seemed to gravitate toward the boys just as they had, she whispered, "Miriam."

Timneet paused. From the corner of her eye, she watched Miriam turn away from the bodies and face her.

The bodies of their friends, this loss of life and separation, their bleak future was too much for Timneet. She closed her eyes, fearing a reaction she could not bear to see. "I'm leaving," Timneet whispered. A few silent seconds later, she slowly opened one eye followed by the other and faced Miriam who did not question when, where, or how her best friend was to escape. Timneet watched as a comforting smile took over Miriam's face.

"Did you hear me, Miri?" Timneet asked, confused by her friend's look of happiness. "I'm joining the movement to free Eritrea," she whispered.

Miriam took a moment before replying and looked to the sky. She lowered her head and closed her eyes as tears streamed down her face. When she opened them again, she asked a question Timneet hadn't expected to hear. Miriam wiped her face with her other hand and asked, "When do we leave?"

Chapter 3

Narrated by Ma'arinet Neguse

We shape our dwellings, and afterwards,
our dwellings shape us.
—Winston Churchill

"It's a 505 area code." Esak's voice shook, but I was more distracted that the week old device in our home had allowed him to know a call had even come in.

"Where in the world is *that*? You're really putting that caller box to use!" Esak's employer, Line Central Atlantic, was running a trial for something called "Caller ID," and we reaped the benefit of having one of our very own in our apartment, decorating our narrow kitchen countertop. It was a device expected to hit homes nationally in a few years. In 1989, though, calling someone's home and being identified within the first few rings by name *and* number was a ridiculously far-fetched idea. It was right up there with flying cars and men bearing children.

"It's Albuquerque. It came up on the screen as, 'NM Corrections.' I think it's her, Maari. I, I think she's back." With one line, everything changed.

"Aw jeez, Ees…," I sighed. My heart sank for him, burning even as it dropped to the depths of my stomach where it floated in acid. I knew exactly who *she* was, but I avoided bringing any attention to her name, as though if spoken, it would transmit some life-ravaging disease, like leprosy. Yes, Terar had *that* kind of effect.

"When did the call come in?" I asked.

"Five minutes ago. I almost picked it up. Maari…I know it's her."

A huge drug bust in New Mexico made national headlines the week before. More than one-hundred East Africans and Central Americans were captured in one of the largest sting operations in the nation's history. Esak's biological mother, Terar, a woman who had spent more time in prison for drug trafficking than raising her four children, lived in Phoenix, Arizona. Phoenix was less than a day's drive to Albuquerque. Esak and I both knew what one plus one equaled—too much Terar.

"You don't know it's your mother for sure." I heard the attempt to sugarcoat hell leave my mouth ever so effortlessly and I wondered if he believed me. I surely didn't.

"Don't call her that," he snapped. "She's never been one."

"Ees, calm down. You don't even know if it's Terar." I shuddered at the sound of her name, praying my skin wouldn't suddenly crowd with lesions.

"Maari, I think she's trying to reach out to me again."

"How would she even have our home phone number?"

"She might have called my mom and dad." Terar had given Esak's adoptive parents, Mr. and Mrs. Connor, a large dose of grief the last time she phoned, and the thought of her calling causing a ruckus from jail again did not surprise me in the least bit.

"Ees, your parents would *never* give her our phone number." We were both lucky to have parents who weren't biologically ours bless us when and how they did. It was the reason Esak and I understood each other so well.

"I don't know. I just have a gut feeling she's back." He spoke what I felt.

That woman traveled in and out of her children's lives faster than changing winds. I was only present for one year of it, the year we had been courting. I'll never forget our first date when he put the secret of his stormy past on the dinner table—literally, pictures of his mother in an orange jump suit next to my plate of chicken and a framed photo of his father's casket beside my mashed sweet potatoes.

"Please deposit 25¢ for the next three minutes," the automated pay phone operator interrupted, cutting the tension.

I spoke fast. "Listen, I don't have any more quarters. I'll be home right after class. Be strong Ees." I repeated the encouragement in Tigrinya with one of the few words he knew and loved, *"Ajokha."*

"Please deposit 25¢ for the next three minutes."

"Thanks Maar." Esak's voice shook more than before.

I felt a little guilty for not being able to stay on the phone and listen to more of his suspicions, but the dial tone could not have come at a more perfect time. My wristwatch read 9:27AM which meant I had three minutes to get to my second class, nearly half a mile away. My legs would need a major recovery afterwards, having gone through the traumatic experience of carrying my one hundred and seventy pounds with the attempted speed of an Olympian.

Why is everything so far away when you're late!

The Mennepf Arts building on Steaton University's west campus always smelled like mold. As I entered its halls to get to my photography classes, especially in the heat of the summer, I made the *I just got a whiff of spoiled milk two weeks past the expiration date* face, forcing me to halt in my tracks and collect myself. My face didn't stay contorted for very long, though. A set of eyes caught my attention, staring at me as I made quite possibly the ugliest expression he had ever seen. I headed in his direction toward my classroom, slightly embarrassed. He looked away, obviously not wanting to seem like he was gawking at me. He wore a White Sox baseball cap and a Cubs t-shirt, and as I walked closer and he looked my way again, I noticed the latter matched the blue in his eyes.

You're sporting rivals? Rival teams from the same city? I thought. I pictured him at the bookstore down on Canal Street, hand-picking articles of clothing representing a number of Chicago sports teams, while choosing sizes that accommodated his extra broad shoulders and massive legs. I would've bet top dollar he had either a bull, a bear, or the profile of a Native-American embroidered on his briefs. Die-hard Chicagoan *wannabes* were everywhere since Michael Jordan was drafted a few years earlier.

"Mornin'." He shifted his three enormous textbooks to one arm and tilted the bill of his cap, bowing his head as he walked passed me, like a cowboy out of an old western film tipping his hat to greet the dainty ladies before him.

"Hi, how's it goin'?" I asked as we crossed paths, not expecting nor waiting for a response.

There's no way he's from here. I turned around to watch him as he walked away. His head bobbed from one classroom number to another.

"Excuse me." It was a bit forward of me, but there was something about him, maybe his manners, that urged me to offer a little guidance. "Where are you trying to go exactly?"

He sunk his shoulders, apparently relieved. "I'm looking for Room 50, a class called 'Capturing Photography'? You don't by any chance know where that is, do you?" he asked as he winced, seeming hopeful that he may have reached someone with an answer.

"Ahh, you're in luck," I said. "I'm headed that way myself."

"Thank you so much. This place is a *maze*." He quickly examined the three stories above us.

"I know what you mean. It took me months last year before the day came when I didn't have to ask for directions. The good news is we're walking in together, so hopefully," I searched my class schedule for the professor's name as we speed walked, "ummm…Rosenbaum won't be too hard on us."

We reached our classroom door and peeked through the section of rectangular glass.

"This is it right here. Looks like they've already started." My chest was aching, heart pounding erratically, and my legs suddenly felt like I had been shot with a tranquilizer. "I hate being late," I told my hallway friend. Walking into class tardy on the first day of classes screamed, *please remember me for the rest of the semester*, and there was nothing more I despised.

"Me, too," he agreed. "Hey, I owe you." He was beaming and it was contagious, enough to settle my worries. He shifted his books to open the door for me, and I returned the gesture by holding it for him.

All thirty-some pairs of eyes turned to the right of the classroom, including a disinterested Rosenbaum. The professor returned to his roll sheet. While my hallway friend and I stood in the doorway scanning the room for empty seats, I heard my name on the chopping blocks.

"Mar—mar—aar—ara—n—whew. I'm going to need help with this one." Rosenbaum slipped his reading glasses down to the tip of his nose and searched the classroom for the person attached to a name much too difficult to pronounce. I wanted to disappear.

"It's Maarinet like clarinet, last name Neh-goos-eh I'm here." The words darted from my mouth in one breath, my hand shooting up in the air and back to my side just as swiftly. I pronounced it without the apostrophe in my name, something I always did when I didn't want to go through explaining that my name was made of sounds their throats and tongues weren't trained to make. My hallway friend and I ducked between the class and the overhead projector as we made our way to a few empty chairs on the far left side of the room.

"Very well. Nice of you to join us, Maarinet." Rosenbaum offered no smile to suggest any sincerity in his welcome. "Jackson Phillips...Sara Porter...Amanda Reeves...Patricia Rogers...Jonathan Sears...," he continued.

Just once, I would have liked my instructor to read my name correctly and move on to the next student without any hesitation. When I was younger, I repeatedly asked God during prayer why He couldn't have given me a name like Jessica or Michelle, a name that didn't cause my second grade teacher Mrs. Hudson, someone who in my eyes knew everything about the world and everyone in it, frequent amnesia.

"Samantha Stein...Reid Stone—"

"Here, sir," my hallway friend raised his hand.

Reid Stone, what a strong name, I thought.

Within minutes, our first assignment was on the wall. I was probably the only student in the room who was thrilled to be getting guidelines for a project on the very first day. We had three options to choose from for our first photography collection piece. Rosenbaum wrote the titles on the transparent sheet:

Scrapers of the Sky
The Earth Moves
Roots to Trees

Chicago was known for its breathtaking skyscrapers, the Sears Tower, John Hancock building, and though not as vertically-astounding, the beautiful diamond shape that outlined the roof of the Smurfit-Stone building or—as my best friend Sarsum was never tired of calling it—its more popular name, the Vagina building. I also loved the Chicago Botanic Garden in Glencoe and the lush grounds of the Baha'i Temple in Wilmette. *Choices, choices,* I thought.

I daydreamed as Rosenbaum explained the instructions for the first two projects, doing everything but listening, including admiring the detail in Reid's gorgeous wedding band.

I wonder if he's polite to her all the time. I wonder if he trusts her. I glanced at his rough blonde beard as he jotted down notes. *Do you make her feel like there's nothing she can say to ease your worries? Do you ask her every day to never leave you? Do you trust her?*

I felt small. Esak continually needed to hear me reassure him of my commitment. His mother had tainted his heart, I was certain of it. So much so that I knew in his eyes, I, as a woman, was capable of abandoning him just like Terar. He questioned my allegiance to test if there was anything he could do that would warrant me leaving him.

"Hey," Reid whispered. "Roll your shoulders back." He imitated my hunched back and forward shoulders. "That's bad posture." He wagged his finger like a grade school teacher, smiling.

"Now onto our final piece, *Roots to Trees.* This project consists of capturing photographs of where you come from and incorporating the people involved in making you into the person you are today. This includes family, friends, teachers in your past. The main focus, though, is exploring your childhood and your development— get it? Development…like film?" Rosenbaum slapped his knee as he laughed. When no one showed any interest in his humor, he finished his thought, clearing his throat amongst the silence, "…and your development into adulthood."

My sixty-some-year-old photography professor continued, "Wonderful, now that we have this all squared away, I'll be placing you into groups of no more than three. Your partnership should be used to share ideas and offer motivation along the way. Take a few minutes and review the guidelines with one another, then make your title selections."

Rosenbaum pointed around the room and assigned group members in the most random fashion.

"You two, our latecomers," Rosenbaum smiled as he spoke this time, "you will be our only group of two."

"Hi, I'm Reid," my new partner announced, offering me a handshake.

"Hi, hallway friend, I'm Maarinet," I responded, eliminating using the apostrophe in my name again.

Reid chuckled, exposing his perfectly straight teeth. "Forgive me, but that's a tough one. Where's your name from?" he asked in a country accent.

"I'm from Eritrea." I usually followed it with a description of where it was in relation to the other countries in the Horn of Africa, but explaining why he wouldn't be able to locate my country on a map was far too long of a conversation I wasn't necessarily up to having.

"I've never heard of it. Is that South America?"

As dark as I am? I thought. Then again, I had heard the sun smothered Brazilians with lots of kisses, too.

"No, it's northeast Africa," I answered.

"Interestin'. I'm sorry, I still don't think I've heard of it, and I'm a geography buff." His laugh reminded me of my father's and because of it, I chose to be polite.

Looks like I can't avoid it any more, I thought.

"There's an ongoing war between Eritrea and Ethiopia so we haven't actually *gained* our independence quite yet. But…it's coming." I figured if I talked fast, my cheeks would stop burning. It was a hard pill to swallow at times—claiming a country that wasn't actually a country just yet.

"Where are you from?" I asked Reid.

"Born and raised in Shreveport, Louisiana," he shared, throwing an extra southern accent in the state's name.

"I could tell you were from the south the second you laughed. Your laugh even has an accent," I chuckled.

"Thank you, I think?" Reid mocked. "Do you speak another language?"

"I do. It's called Tigrinya." I surprised myself and rolled my *R* unexpectedly, like it was Spanish.

"Whoa. Can you say somethin'?" he was now intrigued. We weren't focusing on the assignment which would've probably made Rosenbaum have a conniption.

"What do you want me to say?"

"Say, how are ya?"

Aside from feeling like a performing circus animal, I enjoyed Reid's company. It wasn't often people took notice of me. I was overweight, my skin was darker than Hershey's darkest chocolate, the kind with the almonds in them like the bumps of acne on my face. Although my hair reached the small of my back, it was always in the same single, boring braid right down the middle.

"How are you is k*emay alekhee* for a woman and *kemay alekha* for a man."

"That's nuts!" Reid leaned forward, as though the ability to speak another language would seep into his brain through diffusion. "Say, I was late today 'cause the roads were packed." His eyes widened like a child at Christmas.

"You're hilarious." I giggled at his excitement. "Ok, that would be, *dongiye selezi makina meli'en abti menghedi.* That's a *very* rough translation for you along with a few non-Tigrinya words, so don't you dare quote me on that."

"Did you just end that with men are greedy?" Reid joked.

"What? No! M*enghedi*…it means road, but some people use it

to describe a journey."

"I was just kiddin' around," he said, his smile growing. "Seriously though, I've always wanted to pick up another language," Reid shared. "I bet people's brains light up when they express thoughts in multiple languages. There's gotta be a connection with the soul somehow. If ever there was a snapshot I would love to take, that there would be it—foreign words enterin' the mind."

Now that, I was not expecting—a philosophical southerner sports fanatic geography buff in a photography class, I thought, throwing all the things I had learned about Reid into one snapshot.

"I agree," I blurted, catching a glare from Rosenbaum. "Speaking of pictures, let's get back to this assignment before he makes his way over here."

Reid agreed with a nod. "So, I assume you're tacklin' *Roots to Trees*?" he asked returning to his notes of guidelines.

"What makes you say that?" I asked, intrigued.

"Why on earth would someone with as rich a culture as yours, an African heritage," Reid straightened his back regal-like, "pick buildings or nature over her own roots?"

"Maybe because I know nothing about my roots?" I revealed. "I was adopted when I was three and found out about it only a few years ago…when I was sixteen." If I was going to get anything out of this project, I figured I'd air out my dirty laundry early like Esak had done with me on our first date with his family album.

"Ok class, our time is nearing the end. Take the last few minutes to exchange contact information and schedule your next meeting outside of class," Rosenbaum instructed.

I tore a piece of paper from my composition book, wrote my name and home number down. As Reid wrote his, he whispered, "Listen, I didn't mean to stir up anything."

I handed my contact information to Reid as he did the same for me. "No need." I stopped him with my hand in the air. "They're demons I'm still battling." I smiled a sham of a smile which I would bet he could see right through.

"Maybe we can stomp them outta you during this?" he questioned, pointing to his notes on the assignment. "Believe me, my story of home needs some unleashing, too."

"Okay," I replied, the tightness on my face relaxing. "How about we meet at the Luchtenstein Library? Next Monday at 5PM work for you?" I asked.

"Are there any questions before we leave?" Rosenbaum asked.

"Yeah sure, works great," Reid responded. He glanced at my bite-size piece of paper. "Hey, you gotta apostrophe in your name?" he asked.

Why am I so complicated? I thought. "Yep. It's really said in four syllables instead of three, the second one being hard to pronounce in English. There's this whole throat thing." I waved my hand in the air like it was bothersome.

Reid laughed, nodding. "Language."

"Yeah," I said, smiling. "Language."

"No?" Rosenbaum yelled over the noise of shuffling feet, "Good day then!"

* * *

I woke up startled from my nap, bolting upright. The alarm clock flashed 12:00 in red. I hadn't fixed the time since the power outage from the night before. The heat waves were destroying the electrical wires in our Midtown neighborhood.

I left my watch on the kitchen counter, I recalled, sucking my teeth in disappointment.

"Ees," I whined loud enough to be heard, "what time is it?"

"It's uhhh," I could hear him fumbling dishes, hesitating. "It's 4 o'clock," he finally answered.

"Dammit, Esak," I yelled back, hurling the blanket off my legs. "Why didn't you wake me up?"

I leapt from the bed and poked my head around the Japanese checkered screen, one of two we used to divide our studio apartment into a bedroom, living area, and kitchen.

"I asked you to make sure you wouldn't forget this time." I turned my attention to the textbooks on our nightstand, sneaking a glimpse of Esak for all of one second through the large cracks of the screens before I started hurling essentials into my backpack. When I finished, I came from behind the divider and walked toward the kitchen. The cold of the tile floor, the one that always made me switch from thin socks to slippers, was missing. Instead, my feet were cushioned. My eyes fell to the floor, walking to each section to see how far Esak had gone. Pink rose petals covered nearly every square inch of our one room apartment.

"Eeeees." The hair on my arms rose as did the pitch in my voice. I hugged myself. "What's all this?" I asked through a wide grin.

"It's for you, sweetheart." He finished washing the last of the dishes, dried his hands with a kitchen towel, and approached me with open arms. At 5 feet 7 inches Esak stood only a few inches above me and kissed me on my forehead.

"I love you," he cooed. Esak tucked my head underneath his chin. A minute went by before he iced the warmth within me and shared his mantra, "Maari, please don't leave me."

"What in the world are you talking about?" I asked, snapping my head from beneath his face.

"I just want you to promise you'll always be by my side," Esak said.

I didn't like it one bit. Talks of his mother always brought about these insecurities, and it was unfair to me. Esak was asking for me to commit to our relationship for the millionth time.

"How often are we going to have this conversation? I'm not going anywhere." I fell into his trap, reassuring him of my love yet again.

"Ok, I just wanted to do this for you." Esak waved his hand around the room, like he was a magician revealing he had made a human being vanish into thin air.

"Thank you, love. I really do appreciate it. It looks beautiful in here. It's even more beautiful in here." I tapped the left side of his chest.

He smiled, exposing the mirrored gap in the center of his upper and lower set of teeth. "Why don't you take a picture of the flowers with your fancy camera? You look extra professional when you use that thing," Esak chuckled.

"Camera—Ees, you just reminded me. I have to go! Reid...," I muttered as I ran back behind the screen, diving for my small cabinet of clothes.

"What? Who the hell is Reid?"

"Remember, I told you about Reid, my partner in my photography class? The married guy." Reid's marital status was stated for good reason. Esak's jealous rants were inevitable at the sound of another man's name, even if it were my own father.

I changed into a pair of black shorts. They fit more snug than usual. *I have got to get this diet thing together and fast. I can't keep giving my clothes away.*

I continued to explain myself. "We scheduled a study session for 5PM today at the library. That's why I asked you to wake me up."

I struggled with the zipper. "Did you run my shorts through the dryer, honey?" I asked, hoping I could blame the extra rolls around my waist on the heat cycle.

"No," Esak mumbled. "Which library?" he asked a little louder.

"Luchtenstein, right across from the art building. Which do you think will get me there sooner, the #81 or the #151?" I rambled on, hoping he would get lost in my words and forget whatever fight he was attempting to start.

"Take the Sheridan bus," he said. "So, you're leaving me to be with another man?"

Esak was a jokester and it was difficult for me to believe anything that came from his lips, but a part of me *did* believe his words this time around.

I found a 2XL shirt, perfect to fit over my muffin top comfortably.

"You're kidding, right?" I emerged from behind the screen again —this time appropriately dressed to leave.

"Yes, I'm joking." Esak lounged on the futon staring at the ceiling.

"Ees, he's married, and not to mention," I put my hands on my hips, "I'm 110 percent taken."

I leaned over, gave him a peck on the cheek, and ran to the bathroom to finish getting ready. I heard Esak jump to his feet, trailing me like a lost puppy—the kind that would not stop barking.

"Married or not, I know how men think, Maari." He spoke to my reflection in the mirror while I opened the cap to my burgundy lipstick and rolled it to the surface. It was my absolute favorite color.

"What do you need all that for? Who are you trying to impress?" Esak asked, growling.

"No one," I said.

"I told you before, that color makes you look like a chain-smoking slave."

I replaced the cap and put the lipstick away without having used it. I had learned that giving in was how you preserved peace.

"You're being unreasonable, and I have to run, Esak. Excuse me." I crouched under his extended arm that formed an arch with the bathroom doorway and searched for my keys and sunglasses back in the bedroom.

"I'll be back before 8PM," I blurted behind me.

"You really need three whole hours to work with this guy on pictures?"

"Why are you always so suspicious of me? And yes, I need all

the hours I can get to focus on my education, if that's fine by you."
My heart was racing irregularly. "Why are you making things so
difficult? Have you seen my keys?" I asked.

"Nope," he answered.

*Who am I kidding? Getting help from a man who would rather
have me strapped to the couch—forever, if he had it his way and it
was legal*, I thought. No more than a minute later, I yelled, "Found
'em! Thanks for your help, Ees." I rolled my eyes. I knew he could
tell I was angry by the way he sulked his shoulders in an *I didn't
mean it* kind of way. It was all so unnecessary.

"Alright then, go," he pouted.

"I'll be back before dark, I promise." Even in my disappointment,
I gave him another peck on his cheek. I grabbed my camera bag and
backpack and ran out of our apartment.

***

The #151 Sheridan bus dropped me off right in front of the library,
on the corner of Sheridan and Eden. Reid sat on the front steps, his
chin resting in his palm while his elbow seemed lost in his thigh.

"Hey, Reid," I called out.

"Hey, Murnet," Reid answered as he turned my way and rose
from the ground.

"Call me Maari," I laughed, shaking my head.

"I'm sorry. Did I just pull a Rosenbaum?" he grimaced, poking
fun at our instructor.

"You're fine," I assured him. "Sorry I'm so late. Traffic was horrible!"

"*Aww*, it's alright. We still have some hours on our hands."

"You're right. Let's get to work," I said, smiling. "Ready to go in?"

"Yes, ma'am." He held the door open, waving me inside. "Hey,
you're not headin' back home on the bus, are you?"

"Yeah, why?" I whispered as we entered the land of the quiet.

"I can take you. I drive." He matched my low volume.

"Very sweet of you, but I'm all the way up north, in Midtown." I pointed to the double doors behind me as though my neighborhood were just outside.

"That's actually perfect. My wife works at Gleiss Memorial over there on Navy Drive. She gets off at 11PM tonight."

"Oh wow, I live just a few blocks from there. I'm in the Sunnyvale building," I said.

"Well then, that settles it." Reid was clearly in no mood for negotiations.

"I have to be home by 8PM though…lots of studying I have to get done." The lie rolled off my tongue as effortlessly as it was to return Reid's contagious smiles. I told Esak 8PM and if I weren't home by then, he would surely throw a fit, especially since I was working alone with another man.

"I was plannin' on leavin' around that time anyway," Reid replied. "We can make it a short session for today."

"Thanks, Reid." I didn't even put up a fight. The Chicago bus transit wasn't exactly the safest on summer evenings. "I'll take you up on that offer."

We found an empty conference room on the fourth floor and settled in.

"My best friend, Sarsum, and I come to this room *all* the time. You can see the sunset from here." I pointed to the wall-sized window that reached from the floor to the ceiling and shared, "It's the only room with padded seating." I put my hush finger to my lips and warned jokingly, "Don't tell a soul."

Reid chuckled before asking, "So, why are you in this class?"

"Well…*Amereeca iz za laand of opportunehtee*, as my parents would say." I threw my hands in the air and looked to my palms the way my parents did when admiring the great potential within the United States. I continued in a more serious tone. "They value what you can make of yourself here, so much so that they insist I become an esteemed doctor or an invincible lawyer."

"And how does that tie in with photography exactly?" he asked.

"I live in the world of photography because I don't share their dream." I tapped the eraser of my lead pencil on the desk. "I was born to be a photojournalist. The day that Eritrea is free, I plan on making a story of the struggle by capturing the post-war devastation and what independence looks like after years of combat. And while I'm there, I'll chronicle my journey of finding answers to my earlier years of life that my parents seem to know nothing about."

"How old are you?" Reid asked.

"Nineteen," I answered. "How old are *you*?" I didn't know what my age had to do with what I had shared with Reid, but I thought I'd ask him the same, anyway.

"Holy smokes! At nineteen I was in n' outta trouble, robbin' grocery stores for fun until I was caught and did a few months in jail. I'm thirty-two."

I saw kids in my neighborhood getting arrested all the time, so Reid's comment didn't necessarily surprise me. "Yeah, well we all have something that makes us grow up faster than others, I guess. Mine was my parents breaking the news of my adoption a few years ago."

"Maari, have you talked with anyone about this? Like a professional?"

"I'm not crazy." I was defensive, grabbing hold of my legal pad and pressing it against my chest. *What was I thinking sharing this with a stranger?* I thought.

"No, no, you don't understand." Reid waved his hands like I had mistaken his intentions. "You just seem a little tense. You must be goin' through a lot. I just wondered if you had ever considered goin' for counselin' to help you sort out anything that could be weighin' you down. There's nothin' to be embarrassed about. My parents put me in counselin' the week after comin' home from jail. My wife and I got pre-marital counselin', and even after we married, we continued, once every few months. It's actually been really healthy for me personally and our relationship."

I heard Reid's helpful suggestions, but I was frozen—sent back in time to the day my parents first told me I wasn't theirs.

"Can you imagine being told, 'We are not your real parents,' and then having to hear about how they know nothing about who your real parents are? All they knew was that they were dead. And do you know what I did when the news first hit my brain?" I pointed to my head.

"What?" Reid asked, hanging off the front of his chair.

"I threw up." I rambled on, "I didn't even know what they meant by *real*. I mean, I thought I knew what the word meant, but I couldn't stop replaying it to see if maybe, just maybe, there was a definition tucked deep in my mind that meant something other than true or actual. I searched hard for something that would replace it and make me feel like my world wasn't crashing down."

"Maari, I don't even know what to say." Reid shrugged his shoulders and kept them close to his ears.

"I don't usually spill like this. I guess this assignment is making me pay closer attention to pent-up emotions that I never really explored."

"Believe me, it's doin' the same for me."

"Really?" I asked. "What's your story?"

"Well…," and as if he were snatching his thought back, as if it were too painful to recall, he said, "you finish first."

I nodded, telling myself to remember to ask him again once I was done. "I remember very little about how I physically returned to the living room, but the conversation that took place once I sat back on the couch with my parents will never leave my memory. It was the first time I had ever seen my father, the most unemotional man I know, sit with streams of tears on his face with no desire it seemed to wipe them away. My mother cried like I had died, and in that moment, a large part of me felt like it actually had."

"Wow," Reid interrupted. "What did they say? How do you even begin with news like that?"

I let the memories flood my mind. "After an hour of silence, of sitting on the couch with my father's arm around me staring at the floor and my mother swaying from side to side in the corner of the room by herself, I asked a question whose answer I wasn't necessarily prepared to hear. I asked them what they meant by real."

I felt a pouring from my soul onto the library table that was liberating. "My father choked on every word and asked me if I remembered Daniel, my brother who passed away as we fled from Eritrea to a refugee camp in Sudan. My father started the story at the beginning when all I wanted was to hear the end. I wanted him to cut to the part that summed it all up in a line or two, but I was too much in shock to make any suggestions."

"Was Daniel really your brother and you both were taken by your adoptive parents? Or was he *their* son?" Reid asked.

"That's exactly what I asked. Every thought was one that questioned the truth behind every *fact* my parents had shared about my life." I continued telling the story as it had been told to me three years ago. "When Daniel died, my mom and dad made an unplanned stop at an orphanage which was operating as a secret shelter for Eritreans on the run to Sudan. They heard the shelter was often attacked by the regime, but it was the only opportunity they had to rest and mourn for Daniel who was their son, not my biological brother. When they arrived, none of the children paid them any attention, except for a three-year-old orphan who walked right up to them as they spoke with the shelter organizer and put her hands out to be picked up."

"That little girl was you," Reid finished my thought.

I nodded. "My parents had both died during the war. No one knew who they were or if they had any relatives."

"How did you get there…to the orphanage?" Reid asked.

"I was dropped off by a nurse who brought me there from the hospital. My parents said that when I approached them, they lifted me up and the woman operating the shelter could not stop praising them as if they had performed a miracle. No one had seen me smile since I was left there, and there I was in their arms, laughing like I was making up for lost time."

Reid whispered, locking his gaze onto me, "So, they buried Daniel and took you to Sudan?"

"That's pretty much it. My parents say I was a sign from God sent to help them heal, and they were sent to rescue me from a shelter that was, one week later, ransacked by the Ethiopian regime who spared not one life, including the life of the shelter organizer. Who knows? Maybe I *was* meant for them, and them for me."

"Oh my God. Maari, they were your guardian angels. Weren't they scared you were gonna start cryin' while on the road, though, and the Ethiopians would find you?"

"I don't think they cared," I said still amazed by my parents' love for me. "You know what they told me when I asked them that? If they were scared?" I continued, not waiting for a response, "They said they believed I had been sent to ease their journey, or *menghedi* as they call it, not disrupt it. They refused to separate from me after I approached them with open arms. No matter how much I tell myself that it was supposed to happen that way, for God to make rescuers out of my parents and myself, I still feel hurt that for a number of years, I was fooled into thinking my parents were really mine."

"Talk about hurt. I felt the same when my wife Drea first got sick." He played with his wedding ring, twisting it around his finger.

"What kind of sickness?" I asked.

Reid fidgeted in his seat, clearing his throat. "Finish your story first," he urged, giving me a smile that seemed forced. Again, he deflected the topic back to me. "How long did it take to go from Eritrea to Sudan?" he asked.

"They tell me it took sixteen days. More than two weeks of walking, traveling only at night."

"By foot? Jeez! I can't even stand drivin' the hour back and forth from school, let alone walkin' however many miles that is." Reid's mouth dropped open.

"My mother said I was so light on her back. We only moved at night and they kept vigil during the day which was the most opportune time for the regime to catch their prey. Even while being overly cautious, my parents said they cheated death often—outrunning patrols or leaping behind bushes just in time or hiding in a stranger's home. They said they tried to think of explanations for the chance that we would be caught, but there was nothing they could have said to spare our lives. Luckily, we reached the camp in Sudan safely, and shortly after, we received refugee sponsorship to come here to Chicago."

"That's beautiful." Reid smiled, holding his chest with one hand as though it really touched his heart.

"It's alright, I guess." I grinned. I knew I was blessed, but I still wished I knew more about my life before the journey to Sudan.

"And what about you?" I asked, remembering Reid's urgent need to distract from his story. "What brings you to photography and which one are you choosing?" I pointed to the notes for our first assignment.

"Well." He swallowed before continuing, "My wife, Drea, doesn't actually work at Gleiss Memorial."

"Where does she work, then?" I asked.

"It's not about *where* she works. I have to pick her up from Gleiss because she's finishing up her rounds of treatment."

"Treatment for?"

"About a month ago, the doctors knocked us off our feet when they told us they found cancer in her breast."

"Oh my God, Reid. I'm so sorry." I covered my mouth with both my hands. I had never known anyone with cancer.

"We're hangin' in there." He cleared his throat again. "I took up photography to get her best and worst days on camera—her idea. When she gets better, I'm gonna have the first exhibit of the art studio I plan on buyin' be all about her and a tribute to survivors. We've gone through hell and back with this thing, and I just want everyone to know, it doesn't *own* you." Reid tapped his fingernails on the table.

"Hey, we don't have to talk about it anymore," I interjected.

"No, no it's okay," he insisted. "I guess I can incorporate all of this into the project. Drea is my beginning and my everything. Here's to *Roots to Trees*." Reid held his hand in the air, mimicking a toast.

"Reid, you are very strong and so is your wife." I didn't know him very well and I obviously didn't know his wife, but I felt they were the right words to say. I looked into his eyes. If he wasn't staring back at that moment, I would have started crying.

A light knocking interrupted our session. Sarsum's face surprised me at the door. I waved for her to enter.

"Reid, this is my friend I was telling you about—Sarsum. Sar, this is Reid."

"*Oooh*, you are *fine*." After knowing Sarsum for my entire life, her mouth's lack of a filter could still make me blush.

"What are you doing here?" I stood up from my seat, nudged Sarsum hard with an elbow to her arm, interrupting whatever fantasy she seemed to be creating in her head.

"Do you mind if I steal her for a quick second?" she asked, clasping my wrist in her hand, like a mother with her child while crossing a busy intersection.

Reid was still blushing from Sarsum's compliment. "Thank you and absolutely not. I don't mind."

"What's wrong?" I asked as Sarsum pulled me into the hallway. We reached the corridor near a shelf of books. "Is everything okay?"

"Are you crazy?" Sarsum blurted. She had barely kept her voice under a whisper, causing stares from a few students at their desks.

"What is *wrong* with you? *What* are you talking about?" I demanded.

"Esak called my house looking for you," Sarsum pouted. "Did you bother to look at your watch while you were in there playing photographer with Fabio?" She flicked the camera around my neck, missing and hitting the center of my chest instead. "It's 8:30PM, Maar."

"Sar, shut up. I'm working on an assignment…and for God's sake, he's *married*," I emphasized. I was more upset with myself for failing to keep track of time.

"Well, you might want to tell your jealous boyfriend that," she retorted.

"Sar, what did he say to you?"

"In so many words, he told me to make sure I get your butt home before he kills you."

"That is not funny," I said.

"And, I'm not laughing. Get your stuff, Maari. Let's go."

I knew those words didn't really come from Esak. Sarsum wouldn't have made me go home had that been the case.

"And, on our way home, I want you to do me a favor and introduce me to your academic advisor—whoever got you into this here photography class."

"Why?" I asked as we walked back toward the cozy room.

"I want the same schedule with fine men and assignments that make me look into another man's eyes, like when I first walked in on you two." Sarsum cracked her favorite mischievous smile.

"You, my friend, are a wild child up here." I tapped Sarsum on the forehead as we continued to walk and I struggled with how to tell Reid I needed to leave and I wouldn't be needing a ride after all.

We reached the meeting room and unrehearsed words flew from my lips without thought. "Hey Reid, I am so sorry. I have to go take care of that studying I was telling you about."

"Is everything else okay, though?" he asked, standing from his seat when we entered the room, wearing a frown so deep that the corners of his mouth nearly touched his chin.

"Yeah, everything is okay. I didn't realize it was after 8PM," I said.

"Oh wow, time flew by. Well, I promised you a ride," Reid said.

"It's alright, I'm driving," Sarsum interjected. Either Sarsum just came from the auto dealership or, the more likely possibility, she was lying to protect me. Esak would surely be waiting by the bedroom window, overlooking Sunnyvale Street. Reid dropping us off was not an option.

I looked at Sarsum while she continued to stare down Reid, giddy as ever.

"Okay, I'll see you tomorrow then?" Reid asked.

"Yes, same time? Same place?" I asked in return.

"Sounds good," Reid answered. He turned to Sarsum. "It was nice meeting you."

"Likewise." Sarsum hid her smile like a timid schoolgirl.

When we reached outside, I let Sarsum have it.

"Sar, you little twerp. As nice as that man is, you're lucky he didn't offer to walk us to *your* car."

Sarsum laughed. "Oh shush, I need to get you home before your man's insecurities eat him alive."

Sarsum may have been my best friend, but I hardly ever spoke of my relationship issues with her. I liked my privacy. It did make me wonder, though. *Is Esak that transparent?*

We ran to the next bus stop on Sheridan Avenue just in case Reid stepped outside and saw us waiting there by the doorsteps of the library.

"Sar," I called as we jogged, "this assignment is like therapy."

"You're gonna need therapy after dealing with Ees if I don't get you back. He's crazy, Maar."

"Watch your mouth—that's my heart, Sarsum, and you know it."

"I don't mean anything by it. Don't pay me any mind." Sarsum ended the conversation.

I changed the topic once we reached the bus stop and I caught my breath. "The reason I was late was because there was an accident with the Sheridan bus, and if he calls you later and asks questions wanting to know details, tell him you were too worried about getting home to your mom that you didn't keep track of any details."

"Ok," Sarsum agreed.

We sat quietly on the way home, like two children out past their curfew awaited by the wrath of African parents and their extension cords.

When I arrived home, I rushed through the front door. "Hey babe," I said, panting. The petals at my feet greeted me before Esak did.

Be normal, I reminded myself.

"You would not believe the craziness I went through tonight to get home to you," I continued, setting my purse in the hall closet, prepared to recite each line about the accident perfectly.

The frames which held photographs I had taken along the Lake Shore Drive beaches rested crookedly on the outside wall of the kitchen. I straightened all four of them, buying myself some time before Esak began his uproar.

I followed the trail of rose petals that greeted my feet to the living room where Esak sat quietly in front of a shut off television.

I should be more grateful. Not fair to repay him like this—have him sitting here with his mind in a frenzy. "Ees?" I called.

Like a zombie, Esak rose and went behind the screen door to be by himself in our bedroom.

I sighed, a little relieved I wouldn't have to hear him yell. Still, there was an eerie feeling in the apartment. Esak never kept quiet when angry. Something was stirring.

Whatever is on that mind of his...it's scaring me.

***

Esak came into our bedroom, fresh out of the shower as I climbed out of bed.

"Ees, I'm so sorry about last night. I know I said I would be home by 8PM, but we just got carried away with our assignment."

"That's alright Maar," he said as he put on his customer service representative polo shirt. "I was thinking about it last night, and I realized it's pretty simple. You just won't see him again."

"Ees, that's nonsense. Reid is my partner and I have to complete this assignment."

"I don't care. Tell your professor you can only have a girl partner." Esak's face was as serious as a militant.

"A girl partner?" I laughed aloud. "Ees, I'm not five. You're over-reacting."

"No, I'm not. You shouldn't be out late at night with some other man," Esak voiced.

"Ees, I understand I was an hour and a half late, but there was the bus accident..."

The phone rang, saving me from elaborating on a lie I didn't have to tell. We both looked its way.

"Are you going to see who it is?" I asked.

Esak sauntered over to the kitchen countertop.

"It's Stone, R. Who is that?" he shouted.

"That's Reid." I ran to pick up the call.

"Hello?" I answered, feeling Esak's eyes attacking the back of my head.

"Hey, Maari." I heard Reid's voice on the other end, less upbeat than the last couple of times we had spoken.

"How's it going?" I asked, a bit concerned.

"Not so hot. Drea isn't feeling well."

"I'm so sorry." I looked at Esak, wishing he knew what I knew about Reid's wife. Maybe it would make him reevaluate his insecurities. "What's wrong?" I asked.

"Side effects, but I'll spare ya details. Do you mind if we reschedule?"

"Not a problem! I'll just use the time to work on this whole *roots* thing. I hope Drea feels better."

"Thanks, Maari. I'll see you in class tomorrow."

I hung up and turned toward Esak. "See, you got what you wanted. I won't be seeing Reid today. Ees, his wife is sick... with cancer."

"Maari," Esak began, "you're never going to leave my side, right?"

"Did you even hear what I just said? How insensitive can you be? I just told you the man's wife has cancer and you're worried about *yourself*? I'm not going through this with you every day. Just stop it, already. I'm not repeating myself." Disgusted, I asked, "Where's your faith in me?"

"Just assure me and this is the very last time," Esak promised like he always did.

"There will never be a *last* time," I snapped.

I marched out of the room and locked myself in the bathroom. I jumped out my clothes and into the tub, running scorching water over my face, giving my tears a place to hide.

They say relationships take work, but I don't think this is the kind of work they were referring to. How can this be good if it weighs so heavily on me?

The constant doubt was too much to bear, and it made me think aloud, "Will there ever be a day when Esak will trust me and make me feel as though my word is as good as gold?"

I emerged from the bathroom in my towel, landing in the bedroom. The apartment was quiet. Esak had left for work and I found myself in such a state of serenity. I took advantage of the calm in the house and dropped down to the foot of the bed.

"Lord, thank you for loving me. Things are extremely difficult, and I'm calling on you to help me through this. I'm torn, Lord. If this is where you want me to be, then why do I feel so low? Am I supposed to rise above the now, the pain, the heavy burden on my heart, and nurture Esak back to love? Guide me, Lord. Let me know what you want me to do and I'll jump to fulfill it."

The phone rang just as I uttered, "Amen." I hurried, hoping to hear from Sarsum, or even Esak telling me he was ready to get his head examined and that he realized he wasn't normal. I just wanted to be in good spirits.

The Caller ID read "Gergis, Neguse." "Thank you, Lord," I mouthed to the ceiling.

"Ma'arinet," my mother, Nigisti, sang on the phone.

"Hi, Mom! How are you?"

"Very good, Ma'arinet, my love. Me and your *fahzer* want to know if you still come home for your homework."

"Yes, Mom. The only thing I need you to do is dress up in your *zuria* and Dad can wear his *kidan habesha*. The point is to get you in your traditional clothing, so that I can present this as part of home for me. Home wearing home kind of thing."

"Ok, good, I'm get Neguse and we ready for you when you come."

"Great, Mom. I'll be there in half an hour. Love you."

"Love you too, *za gwalay*." There was something about the way my mother called me her daughter in Tigrinya that made me feel like I belonged in this world.

I dressed quickly and walked to the bus stop on my way to explore home from behind a lens. *First stop*, I thought, *King Drive where I walked to and from elementary school every day as a little girl.*

When I arrived, I sat on the stoop of a padlocked pawn shop on 73rd and King Drive and snapped away. The buzzing coming from the store sign overhead sounded like a swarm of flies zapped with electrical currents forcing them to stop breathing every other second. The spurts of humming continued, but my concentration remained unbroken. The women at the bus stop surely thought I was insane, in the middle of the projects with a camera as large as mine out in the open for all to see. Little did they know, I grew up on these streets. I felt their eyes burning into me as I daringly took pictures of passersby. When their stares became even more piercing, I removed my head from behind the camera and gave the pair my undivided attention.

"Hi, ladies," I waved, raising my eyebrows, "do I look familiar to you?" The children's storyteller voice I used made me chuckle inside. *In other words, stop staring at me*, I thought.

If the sun weren't so uncomfortable, beaming directly on the bus stop where the women stood wiping the sweat from their foreheads and waving cool air to their faces from paper fans, I would have moseyed over to them and introduced myself in all of my sarcasm.

"Careful with that picture box, girl. Somebody 'round hea'll snatch it," the nice woman said.

"Doris, mind yo' business," her friend warned, smacking Doris on the sleeve of her fuchsia colored blouse.

"I don't want the chil' hurt, Jenetta," Doris explained, shooing her friend with the flick of her wrist.

"Appreciate you ma'am, really I do." *There I go again. Why is my mouth so big?* I thought.

They turned back around toward the street.

I had been sitting there for what felt like hours, waiting for a spectacle to drive, ride, or walk by. I strived to capture the wild side of the streets for one reason—it was my norm growing up. These streets were a version of home for me. Assignment or not, I lived for mornings like these—just my lens and me. It was what mattered most to my heart.

The buildings surrounding the King Drive bus stop barely stood upright. They were just dilapidated apartments but the contrast of their crumbling red brick, the blue sky, and their black windows was breathtaking.

Click.

On one side of a home, garbage bags billowed from several first floor windows. *Home invasion*, I thought, feeling deeply saddened. If glass didn't stop the burglars, neither would plastic. A burly man entered my lens, and I followed him to the window. Zooming in, I focused on the hammer and a row of steel bars in his hands. I wanted to shout words of praise for this homeowner taking matters into his own hands.

Click.

Zip codes on this side of the city appeared no different than war zones. Years of neglect caused roofs to cave in. But, an image surfaced that turned my sadness into overwhelming joy—laughing children infiltrated my lens, and they weren't even aware of the target lines on their smiles.

Click.

In my photographer eyes, beauty would always live here, despite what the city and renovation coordinators felt about the south side of Chicago.

"*I live in a world...in a world of my own,*" a deep voice sang, booming from down the street. I quickly exchanged rolls of film. I had never been to a blues club, but I certainly knew the melody when I heard it.

"What in the world?" Doris failed to restrain herself, and the pair burst out in giggles like a pair of schoolgirls relentlessly poking fun of the least popular girl throughout the year. I knew what it felt like to be on the other side of those jeers, and I knew it well.

"*Yes, it's mine…all mine in my head.*" The singing grew more soulful but less skilled in pitch.

Click.

"What is *this*?" Jenetta roared as he approached the bus stop. I could hear the disgust in her voice—contempt for the gaudiness of a grown man.

"Jenetta, hush yo' mouth. This foo' crazy!" Doris silenced her friend.

Pink and purple were either his favorite colors, or he had daughters who played dress up with him early this morning. The latter, however, did not explain how he managed to get his hands on an adult purple set of overalls. Something told me he may have worked solo on his image. The pink boa snuggled around his neck, while the bald spots of a Mr. T Mohawk screamed for a towel to wipe the downpour of sweat.

"Hold it…right there," I spoke gently behind my lens.

Click.

He stopped at the red light, and I was amused by the bright colors swaying to the blaring instrumental blues beat from a roped down boom box sitting atop the bike's front basket. It was odd for a cyclist from these parts of the city to stop for a red light. I soon realized the stop was attention-seeking rather than traffic-obeying.

"Nobody can take this world from me
'Cause in the end it's mine
And all I ever, ever had.

So, leave my baby alone with me."

With his front wheel behind the pedestrian walkway, the man looked to his right and acknowledged the two women and myself with a nod.

I kept to a mental space of my own. *What are you doing? Where are you from?*

As if he were trying to ease the confusion in me he said, "It's so my heart can feel it, ya hear?" He stretched his *E* in hear and danced in his cushioned bicycle seat. He alternated pats between the loud box and his chest.

I pushed my shot button like a machine gun, capturing a series of his movements.

Got it. Wow, what a gorgeous smile. I whispered, "I hear you." I would never know what kind of life this man led or what trials he had faced, but in that very moment, our souls smiled together and it was enough to make me feel I understood a perfect stranger. The traffic light turned green and the man was on his merry way.

"See y'all on the other side, where my world is yours and yours, mine," he interrupted his ballad to bid us goodbye. "Ha ha!" he laughed at his creative rhyme, giving himself a high five. A final flick of my finger and I caught the last flash of waving pink from the back of the unforgettable man on his loud bicycle.

Now that is one happy soul, I thought. Despite a world that would never quite understand his choice to flamboyantly express his inner glee, the man was unstoppable.

"Time to explore, my home, home," I whispered.

***

"How is *zis* one, Ma'arinet *gwalay*?" My mother jumped in front of the door with the zeal of a costumed child on her way to trick-or-treat.

"Mom, that's beautiful!" Her *zuria* was stunning, a cream-colored traditional gown, embroidered with a gold and black design down the middle and along the hem of the dress.

"Your *fahzer* buy for me," my mother announced, twirling into the living room designed in Eritrean décor. Cow hides, with paintings at their center, furnished empty spaces on each wall. The coffee pot, or *jebena,* awaited me in the middle of the living room, along with three *finjal* for my mother, father, and me to sip from when the coffee was ready.

"*End* he buy *anozer* one for you, too." My mother outstretched her arms and revealed my new dress.

"Wow! Thank you, Mom!"

"Don't *sank* me. I did *nuhsing. Sank* your *fahzer!*" she urged.

My father, the tallest man I knew at 6 feet 4 inches tall, walked into the room decked in white from the tip of his hat down to his patent leather shoes.

"Bellisimo!" my mother exclaimed as her husband entered the room.

"*Sank* you, *sank* you." My father swayed from side to side, imitating the stiffest fashion model on a runway.

"Dad, you look amazing!" I immediately grabbed my camera dangling from my neck and snapped frame after frame. "Okay you guys, I want this to be as natural as possible, no posing, *heriy?*"

"*Heriy, heriy.*" My mother repeated in English as though it would reassure me more, "Okay."

"What is *po-sing, za gwalay?*" My mother asked as she pulled my father next to her and stood rigidly, smiling for the series of flashes.

"Just be natural, Mom. In other words, don't look at the camera. Go to your *jebena* and start brewing coffee, if you would?"

I let my parents settle in their seats before revealing what was really on my heart. "Dad, you know how photography has been a passion of mine since the day you let me take pictures with your

Polaroid? Remember when I used to sit there and fan the pictures and get so impatient waiting for your faces to show up? I would jump in the air. Do you remember that?"

My dad chuckled, nodding his head.

"Mom, Dad…I have the best news." I waited for their reaction to change, and when it didn't I carried on anyway. "I know exactly what I want to do with my life."

My mother beamed and clapped her hands, rising from her stool and leaving her *jebena* atop the portable stovetop to snuggle next to my father on the couch, asking, "Which one do you think she'll choose? I wonder, doctor, lawyer?"

This is going to be difficult. I just have to blurt it out. It's like ripping off a bandage, I thought.

My father interrupted, "Engineer."

"Mom…Dad…photography is my passion. I am going to contribute so much to the whole world." I outstretched my arms as my camera dangled from my neck. "Money isn't everything. I can live with very little of it as long as I'm doing what makes me happy. Please understand how much I want to do this professionally, what I love to do most. I'm an adult now. This is my choice." I ended, less firmly than I had planned.

My words were jumbled, nothing like I had rehearsed. My throat became severely and noticeably dry. My parents had not uttered a single word. They wore blank stares, expressionless.

I excused myself to get a cup of water and when I returned, I realized my parents had not moved an inch. I asked, "Is everything alright?"

My mother turned to her husband for his reply, and my father refused to take his eyes off of me. I had crushed their dream by dismissing their plans for me to become what the Eritrean community of Chicago had predetermined were the most suitable careers for their children. My father stood up from his seat and looked me square in the eyes.

"You want to take pictures?" my father shouted at the very top of his lungs, something he hadn't done in ages. I think he startled himself.

He dropped his grey-haired head in his hands and mumbled words that I thanked God I was unable to comprehend. Within seconds, my mother disappeared into the master bedroom, making her lack of support clear while my father continued his rant, pacing from one end of the room to the other. He soon stopped only an inch from my face to deliver his point effectively.

"What about *everysing* we plan for you? You *are* going to be doctor or lawyer...or *boz*. *Zat's* it!"

I wasn't shocked, but I had hoped my news would have been taken with less disdain.

With my father's final word, he stomped his way to their bedroom, as loudly and as quickly as an older man was capable of doing. He flung his hands in the air in disapproval as he continued down the hallway of walls decorated with framed photos and my gifts to them of their favorite—animals on the streets I had captured on film over the years. He removed each frame from the wall, piece by piece as he neared their bedroom screaming, "No *peecture*! No *peecture*!"

My eyes welled. Disapproval was one thing, but being downright callous was another. When he was out of sight, I composed myself and heaved a sigh, plopping down on the couch. I had experienced my parents blowing discussions out of proportion many times, especially when my desires did not coincide with their plans.

When the bedroom door reopened, I winced, bracing myself. My mother stormed down the hall, louder as she got closer to me. She held an object in her hand. "Here!" she yelled, throwing a disposable camera in my lap. "Play *wiz zis end* stop being fool. You stop right now!" She widened her eyes and stood over me, all 4 feet and 4 inches of her, and pressed her thumb over her folded index fingernail of the same hand, making the shape of a circle. The other three fingers stuck together as though they were a brigade, straight as an arrow. My mother flicked her wrist up and down as though she were chopping an onion. She warned, "Stop *zis* now!" She made her exit as powerfully as my father.

Click.

In the heat of the moment, I took pictures of my mother in her flowing dress as she stormed down the hallway to reunite with my father. "This is what stubbornness looks like," I whispered.

I flipped the camera around.

Click.

"And *this*…this is the look of disappointment."

These are my parents, I thought, chuckling. I had been through this process numerous times while growing up, and as an adult, I understood that new concepts were not really welcome in our home.

The grandfather clock in my parents' living room, the one with the owl for the thin minute hand, *hoo'd* as it struck the top of the hour. "Oh no," I sank in my chair. It was 8PM. My stomach turned. Esak was probably waiting for me at home. I threw my belongings together and made a dash for the door.

***

That night, I walked into a dark apartment. I looked to my right, where my only source of light was the refrigerator door left ajar. It allowed me to see Esak sitting on a folding chair, his back against the wall over to my left.

"Ees?" I called.

Esak sat with his forearms resting on his thighs and his hands in prayer form, pressing his lips in between.

"Ees, what's wrong?" I dropped my purse on the floor, and as

I hurried toward him, the crunching of glass beneath my sandals slowed my steps, sending a sensation of ice up my spine.

"Ees, talk to me!" I shrieked. "What's with the glass on the floor? Are you okay?" I searched his hands for cuts and blood. *Someone's died*, I thought. It was the only explanation I could think of.

"She called again today, crying and asking for money for an attorney."

"Oh my God," I said. Before I could comfort him with encouraging words, his fingernails clawed into the crease of my arm. "Let go of me," I whimpered. He pierced my skin, digging into my bicep.

"Where were you when she was begging? Huh? Having the time of your life with another man, right?" Alcohol saturated his tongue. Esak pulled me down hard to my knees. At least a dozen Heineken bottles rolled around the floor, rattled by the disturbance. He forced his nail deeper as if he wanted to tear my flesh open.

"I was at home with my parents." I struggled against his grip until I looked into his glassy eyes. Fear paralyzed me. "You're scaring me. Esak, you're hurting me." I steadied my voice, not wanting him to match my level of frenzy.

He pushed me off, leaving the seat he occupied and paced wildly just outside the kitchen and into the living room.

"Was that really him that called earlier? Or did you just act like it was him?" Esak asked.

"I know what this is about." I came to the realization as I lifted myself from the ground and onto the seat Esak had just emptied. I brushed the glass from my jeans and watched him pace back and forth. "You think I'm going to abandon you like your mother. Is that it?" They were words meant for myself. They should have never been spoken aloud.

The next minute of my life played like a broken VCR—an unwanted slow motion. Within one leap, Esak was an inch from my body as I nursed my arm.

"I told you to never in your life call her that," he growled. He took an open palm to the side of my face. There was enough force in his angry hands to knock me off the chair and to the ground. He stumbled his way behind the screen to our bedroom, muttering, "Dogs stay on the floor..."

My cheek and jaw throbbed deep into my bones, rendering more pain than a swarm of stinging bees. My eyes shared a stream with my face as I rested my head near a bed of broken glass. I sobbed alone in the dark.

Esak never came to check on me...not once.

CHAPTER 4

The course of true love never did run smooth.
—William Shakespeare

"Zeh dog wok to zeh shope. Rehpeet, class."

Memhir Petros, dressed in a yellow-stained collared shirt un-buttoned to the middle of his chest, whirled to face Timneet's sev-enth grade class. All ten of the thirteen-year-old girls struggled to keep still, shifting their weight on the logs that formed their seats. It was the second hour of lessons and without a break to relieve their behinds, there was plenty of fingernail biting and toe tapping throughout the classroom.

"Zeh dog wok to zeh shope," the schoolgirls echoed.

Memhir Petros pointed to the chalkboard at the third row of English words with the same slender stick he used to strike the knuckles of those who failed to give him their undivided attention. Timneet had already received a warning this morning as she sat in the back of the room whispering into Miriam's ear behind the high bench that reached their shoulders. It was a resting place for an open book of English phrases that neither Timneet nor Miriam was interested in following. Their tongues rejected the lesson of the morning once more and rolled in the familiar sounds of Tigrinya instead, while Memhir Petros gave his back to the class.

"Zeh dog end zeh cat…"

"Can we trust your mother's friend?" Timneet whispered. She was thrilled when she first learned that Miriam had a connection who would lead them directly to the training grounds of the liberation effort. But one week into planning their great escape, Timneet had begun to question their guide-to-be. For one, she had never met him, and Timneet found it hard to trust a man she had never seen. "Are you certain Abo Solomon will take us straight there?" she asked.

"Of course we can trust him. Have faith in him, Timneet…and in me." Miriam abruptly stopped as Memhir Petros spun toward the girls again.

"Rehpeet, class," Memhir Petros instructed.

"Zeh dog end zeh cat play wiz each ahzer…," the other girls repeated. Timneet and Miriam followed the lead of their classmates.

"Zeh dog end zeh cat end zeh chicken…" Memhir Petros turned to the board and pointed to a longer sentence.

"Does Abo Solomon even take people our age? How can you be so certain that he will not object in the end when we will have already run away to meet him?" Timneet raced the words to Miriam's ear, keeping a vigilant eye on Memhir Petros' back.

"Timnet, Abo Solomon was a long-time friend of my mother's. I can trust him. But, there's something I must tell you," Miriam shared.

"What is it?"

"He has advised that we not leave for another month."

"Another month!" Timneet yelled, her fist slamming the log.

"Timneet!" Memhir Petros returned to Tigrinya. "I have already warned you. Do you want the stick to be your friend?" He stabbed his teaching tool into the air toward the back of the classroom.

"Please forgive me, Memhir Petros," Timneet whispered, lowering her head under the bench.

"One more word and your hands will be punished," he threatened.

Timneet nodded, but Miriam's news brought about a pounding pain to her head much too strong to ignore.

"Zeh dog…," Memhir Petros continued with his lesson, turning his back once more.

"We'll be dead in another month," Timneet snarled. "I knew I should have found someone to take us myself." She folded her arms beneath her chest in protest.

"We will die if we choose anyone other than Abo Solomon, I can guarantee you," Miriam responded.

"Why so long?" Timneet asked.

"There is conflict in Sembel, a group of civilians, not freedom fighters, resisting the regime. Abo Solomon says the patrols will be heavy for a little while, so we must wait."

"Rehpeet, cl—," Memhir Petros began. "Girls!" he shouted

Why did you take your eyes off of him? Timneet scolded herself.

She clenched her fists, imagining the beating to her hands to feel the same as when it had burned like fire the last few times she was called to Memhir Petros' desk. Timneet followed Miriam's eyes over the bench, only to find Memhir Petros' attention devoted to a different part of the room.

"One more word and I will send you to the regime. Is that your wish?" Memhir Petros warned the three chattering half-sisters with different mothers, the real troublemakers of the school. The half-sisters obeyed and sat still, which was not the easiest task while on the log.

"They have no manners," Miriam gossiped.

"Leave them alone, Miri. I like them. Tell me, what is our next move, then?" Timneet asked.

"Rehpeet!" Memhir Petros bellowed.

Before the class had a chance to fulfill Memhir Petros' instruction, two patrols stomped their way through the room's missing door, one of them limping as he marched. The men held two boys each by their collars and were trailed by three others.

Timneet had never seen the soldiers. They were not the same faces responsible for the massacre. She looked at Miriam, who had clasped her hands in prayer form and bowed her head, shutting her eyes. Timneet's right eye fluttered and a spell of spins overwhelmed her.

Lord, what now? Timneet thought, her arms crossed and locked onto her stomach, pressing firmly to keep from vomiting.

"We have an announcement," the soldier with the limp exclaimed. They shoved the boys in front of the class where they stood like slabs of meat to be sold, their chins at the top of their chests. "These are your *new* classmates. You girls should tell them what happened to the old boys and make sure they behave. You *may* be able to save them!" the soldier exclaimed.

The patrols slapped the boys' backs, sending them farther between the split logs, to the center of the classroom. "Find a seat," the soldier with the limp roared while his colleague tapped a large club on the ground. As the boys settled in their seats, the soldiers left the classroom, snickering on their exit. "Save them!" the mute soldier gained a voice, repeating his partner's words, cackling along the way.

A boy with swirls of cinnamon in his curly locks sat at the very edge of Timneet and Miriam's log.

"Boys, please find partners near you to share a book. We are learning English. Do any of you know English?" Memhir Petros asked. As if instructed to do so, the boys lowered their eyes to their laps in unison.

"Miri, look at him," Timneet whispered. "He is beautiful." Timneet caught glimpses of his beautiful dark skin out the corner of her right eye.

"He's nothing special," Miriam answered. "Concentrate, now about the plan…"

"Are you even paying attention? Look at his hair, his cheeks." Timneet's eyes grew wider the more glances she stole. A throbbing reached her heart, and the room suddenly fell deathly silent. She heard nothing but the boy's breathing.

"Yes, but would he save your life like Samson?" Miriam smirked.

Miriam shared often that she had always wished Samson and Timneet would spark a romance, but Timneet never had the nerve to tell her best friend that Samson was more like an older brother, like Amaniel, than anything else. Although it was for their protection, Samson was too controlling about places the girls should avoid and what they should wear. In Timneet's heart and for this reason, he was quickly ruled out as a possible boyfriend.

"You haven't even given him a chance." Timneet lowered her voice even more to keep from being heard. "Did you see his eyes when he sat down?"

"Don't play with that boy's heart like that. It will never last, Timneet. We have bigger plans," Miriam reminded her.

"Well, I can make it last for one whole month, can't I?" Timneet smiled. Abo Solomon's delay may have been exactly what Timneet needed.

"Class, turn to the next page," Memhir Petros ordered.

"Come here," Timneet urged the boy, waving him closer. "You can share with us." The boy obliged and scooted near Timneet who took a sudden interest in the subject matter. "Do you know English?" Timneet asked.

"No, we didn't learn it in our school," the boy answered. Timneet had never seen a cleft chin before, making the boy more intriguing than anyone she had ever met.

"Where did you come from?" Timneet's curiosity blossomed, her heart calming from the panic the soldiers evoked. She fought the urge to put her fingers through his soft-looking hair, far more fine than her own coarse hair she forced into three hanging, yet motionless, braids each week.

"Barka," the boy answered.

"All the way from Barka, that's a long walk to make to Zigib every day." Timneet calculated the kilometers, widening her eyes at her conclusion. The route was at least an hour each way. "What is your name?" Timneet asked.

"Ne'Amin," he replied. "And yours?"

"It's Timneet, and this is Miriam." Miriam would not look in their direction, seemingly captivated by the words on the chalkboard.

"Did they tell you where the other boys of this school went?" Timneet whispered.

"Timneet, you cannot keep your mouth closed!" Memhir Petros growled, stomping toward them, where the lucky trio were the only students who had the support of the back wall.

Ne'Amin raised his hand and intercepted Timneet's punishment. "Forgive me, it was me. I was only asking her questions from the book."

Timneet looked to Memhir Petros and nodded in agreement.

"If you have any questions, you ask me. Do you understand?" Memhir Petros said, more understanding toward the newcomer.

"Yes, I understand. Please, forgive me," Ne'Amin muttered.

Timneet looked to Ne'Amin, her heart melting and her eyebrows dropping in gratitude. *Thank you,* she spoke with her eyes. Ne'Amin's eyes stared back with a softness that seemed to say, *I would do it again.*

Timneet turned to her best friend and thought, *You see, Miriam? He would save me.*

When Memhir Petros finally excused them for their twenty

minute break, the sun outside brightened Timneet's mood even more. It was either the sun or the new arrivals. The boys stood in a huddle near the pole of a high-flying Ethiopian flag, separate from the girls who banded together in pairs, or in the troublesome sisters' case, a group of three. Ne'Amin stood apart from the boys.

"Miri, I'll join you in a minute."

"Come on, Timneet. Let's go." Miri pulled Timneet's arm in the direction of the tree that was their favorite spot. Its trunk was large enough to hide Timneet and Miriam from the soldiers, its far-reaching branches and plentiful leaves, enough to create shade from the sun. They chose it to be their secret planning grounds. It was their haven, a place where Timneet would learn more about Abo Solomon's promise to deliver them to their own freedom.

But today Timneet felt compelled to take a few minutes and explore a sensation she had yet to identify. "I just want to welcome Ne'Amin to the school and let him know I can help him when he needs it."

"Timneet, I don't think you should get involved."

"Nonsense, Miri. What is the worst that can happen? I just want to be nice like he was to me." Timneet poked her best friend's cheeks pushing them upwards toward her eyes and forcing a smile to match her own.

Miriam giggled. "I'll be waiting behind the tree."

Timneet walked over to the boy slowly. She risked seeming too eager, and to avoid it, she kicked rocks on her way over to Ne'Amin, looking in every direction but ahead at him. When she reached the boy, she found him kicking the dirt floor of the courtyard. Timneet stood in her tracks for a few minutes, a rush of heat attacking her cheeks. She folded her hands, forward of her waist, and swayed them hoping the boy would notice the action from the corner of his eye. And soon enough, he did.

"We're happy to have you, Ne'Amin. Welcome," Timneet said.

"Thank you, Timneet." Ne'Amin was timid, low-voiced. He talked with his hands in his pockets.

"I should be the one thanking you. You saved me from bruised hands." Timneet held her hands in the air, free of the red welts she was accustomed to wearing. Before the massacre, her snide remarks under the rule of Memhir Petros had earned her plenty classroom battle scars.

"It was nothing. You were kind enough to make conversation with me."

Timneet paused, searching for an end to the awkward silence. Ne'Amin found it first.

"Timneet, can I ask you something?"

"Yes?"

"Where are the boys of the school? Why were we brought here?"

What do I say? She stared at the blood stains on the concrete of the school courtyard. *Thank the Lord, they removed the bodies yesterday.*

The silence must have taken too long. Ne'Amin continued, "Do you know?"

"They disappeared," Timneet shared, shrugging her shoulders. *It is the truth,* she reasoned and quickly diverted his attention. "Did you understand what Memhir Petros covered during the morning half of class?"

"Uhh, I…no, that was another question I had for you," Ne'Amin replied. "Would you be willing to help me with the assignments?" he asked.

"I can help you with studying after school when the soldiers are away." Timneet controlled her excitement.

The cowbell rang in the air, sounding the first warning for class to restart in the next few minutes. Ne'Amin, whipped his neck toward the girl with the piece of metal in her hand and scurried into the school.

"No, wait…," Timneet called. *He must've not realized it was only a warning.* Not wanting to gain the attention of the nearby soldiers against the wall watching the newcomers intermingle with the schoolgirls, she whispered, "Oh, never mind."

Timneet sprinted to Miriam behind the tree. "Great news!" she exploded. "I am now Ne'Amin's helper." Timneet skipped in place, in disbelief of her newfound luck.

Miriam chuckled. "I told you once…it will never last. Did *love* make you forget already, Timneet? We have bigger plans for ourselves." Behind the trunk she raised her fist to the sky and said, "We are going to help save our people." Miriam separated her hands and spread them wide apart. "We are going to free an *entire* nation."

Timneet responded, "Of course, I didn't forget," frowning at her unsteady emotions—ecstatic with the blood rushing sensation of her first crush in one minute followed by the hurt of reality and her destiny in the next. "Of course not," she repeated to Miriam for emphasis. *How could I forget?*

***

"Does he have to walk home with us *every* afternoon?" Miriam snuck the words to Timneet's ear.

It had been two weeks since the boys had become their new classmates and Timneet had promised to tutor Ne'Amin. Miriam had lost any shyness about not wanting Ne'Amin around.

"Miri, you know I agreed to help him catch up and we always have time for one another after he leaves, so what is the real reason you're upset?"

"I think it doesn't make any sense. Soon, you won't even be here to help him, so what does it matter if you help him now or not? In two weeks he's going to be just as lost as when he first came here and what's more, he'll have a broken-heart because you've left. That can't be good," Miriam reasoned.

She made sense, but Timneet heard the twinge of jealousy in her voice.

"Sisters, are you ready?" Ne'Amin emerged from inside the classroom where he had finished collecting more notes from Memhir Petros.

"Yes, we are," Timneet answered, staring sternly at Miriam, warning her to be nice.

"Oh and Timneet, I forgot to tell you. I can't study today, I have to help my mother with a few errands, but I'll walk home with you girls."

"But Barka is in the opposite direction. I understand when we are studying, but when you are going out of your way to walk us home, that may be dangerous for you," Timneet said, expressing her concerns.

"I insist," Ne'Amin demanded, striking his hand through air.

"Alright," she agreed, "but promise me you will be very careful on your way back home?"

"I will," Ne'Amin responded, smiling.

Miriam was jogging a few meters ahead, seemingly giving Timneet and Ne'Amin their privacy.

"How is it that I know nothing about your family?" Ne'Amin asked as the trio made their way past a goat herder and his flock.

"I don't like talking about it."

"Forgive me," Ne'Amin pled.

"The regime…" Timneet choked on her words and decided to not finish her thought. *Go on, tell him. Tell Ne'Amin how they've destroyed your family.* She snapped the side of her dress between her fingers as she searched for the right words.

"Say no more," he interjected.

He understands, Timneet thought, calming her hands by her side.

As they approached the turn of the hill toward the girls' homes, a number of patrols stood surrounding what appeared to be a man on the floor. Their clubs reached above their heads, near their backs, as they swung with full force, beating the man on the ground.

"I have children!" the man cried. "Please!"

Timneet froze in her steps, imagining Amaniel's face as the victim's.

A patrol caught her stares and reached for the gun strapped to his belt. "Move on," he roared from across the road.

Ne'Amin grabbed Timneet by her shirt and scuttled around the corner and up the hill. They sped over the rocks that made up the road leading to Timneet's home, Ne'Amin tightly grasping Timneet's hand. Timneet looked behind her twice. She stopped checking for them when she realized just who she was running from—they were men who would much rather beat a man to death than worry about children.

Miriam must have made it home. How could she have not seen the attack? Maybe she was smart enough to run.

The pair arrived at Timneet's doorstep where they stood staring down the hill before uttering any words.

"Listen," Ne'Amin began. "I wanted to tell you something...this isn't easy for me." He looked from the foot of the hill to Timneet a few more times before stopping his speech.

"What is it? Is something wrong?" Timneet searched his face for clues. "What is it, Ne'Amin?"

"I don't really know how to say this." He shoved his hands into his pockets, looking at the ground. "Thank you for everything you've helped me understand in school. But it's just not the studies..."

Timneet rested her back against her front door and raised his chin with her finger. She met his eyes and urged, "What is it that you are trying to tell me?"

"Timneet, you have my heart. It sings for you." He smiled, revealing a dimple on his right cheek.

"Ne'Amin, I..."

Aregeet's black door of death creaked open, screeching like the sound of a tortured animal. Instinctively, Timneet snatched Ne'Amin by his arm and dragged him into her home. On the other side of the door, Timneet put her finger to her lips and silently warned Ne'Amin to be quiet. She hunched her back with her ear to the door as Ne'Amin stifled his panting, standing perfectly still while his eyes danced from Timneet to the door. When Timneet heard Aregeet's door close again, she sighed a breath of relief.

"Who was that?" Ne'Amin asked.

"She's a spy," Timneet whispered. They stood shoulder to shoulder with their backs against the door facing Timneet's courtyard.

Without a word of warning, Ne'Amin stepped closer, standing nose to nose with Timneet. He pressed her body against the door and gave her virgin lips a kiss. Her body temperature rose and her head teemed with thoughts. Ne'Amin followed the sensual touch with a peck on both cheeks and stealthily made his way out of Timneet's home.

Timneet shut the door behind him, burying her forehead into the metal door while shaking her head. *Why must I leave? Why is this my fate?* she thought. Miriam's voice thundered in her head, quickly dismissing her feelings. *We are going to help save our people. We are going to free an entire nation.*

***

One month had passed. *Any day now, and I will be on the road to joining the freedom fighters.* She straightened her uniform and jogged to the bottom of the hill where for once, Miriam waited for *her.*

"Have you packed your bag?" Timneet asked before bidding her friend a good morning.

"Yes, I have," replied a monotonous Miriam, not displaying the same level of excitement as Timneet.

On their way to school, the road was busy with fleeing chickens from a corner market and sheep separated from their owner as the girls traversed the village of Zigib. They were early this morning. Civilians occupying the roads in herds scurrying to work before the patrols began their watch was a rare sight. Before long, Timneet brushed shoulders with aggressive adults—a change from the uniformed patrols, it made her feel safe. It was as though she were among parents in the crowd, even though they paid her no mind.

"What is wrong?" Timneet asked as they reached the road across the school. Miriam's mouth was rarely shut the entire morning walk. She usually filled Timneet's ears with talk of how she planned on killing every soldier in sight on the battlefield and bringing justice to her mother's name. Timneet knew Miriam was as eager to leave as much as she, but Miriam's silence begged to differ.

"Abo Solomon says we must wait longer."

"For what? For how long?" Timneet wondered if the man even existed. *Maybe Miriam isn't prepared for fighting?* Timneet thought. *Maybe she realizes how much heartache it would be to leave her father and her brother without a woman in the house?*

"Another month." Miriam stretched her words as though she didn't want them to end, while she interlocked her fingers and forced them backwards.

"Are you sick? Sick in the head?" Timneet hissed. "You must be. Every night I am haunted by the screams of the dead. I hear grown men cry like infants. I can't shake the pictures of the hanging dead. And, you...you think I can go on like this? If you think I will stay for another month, you are sick in the head, Miri!"

"Timneet, six boys and three girls were hung in Mai JaJa. Nine our age are hanging by their necks because they followed a guide in the name of joining the freedom effort. If you think you can find someone like Abo Solomon who has the sense to know which roads to avoid and which days to not travel, then tell me who that person is."

"Is he even real?" Timneet asked, running with the suspicion that she had been waiting for a ghost all along.

"Who?" Miriam asked in return.

"Abo Solomon."

Miriam stopped, pounding her fist to her thigh. "He is as real as my mother's ashes."

Timneet took hold of Miriam's hand, immediately regretting her words. "I'm sorry, Miri. I trust you."

"Hello, Miriam." Ne'Amin approached them as the school bell rang a warning. He turned his attention to Timneet, his eyes lighting up like the sun. "Hello, Timneet, my sister." He looked at them back and forth and asked, "Are you ready to go inside?"

Suddenly, one month of waiting didn't seem so bad after all. *If I must stay, at least I'll be in the presence of a boy's love*, she thought.

***

Of the three times Timneet had visited Ne'Amin's home, each time she marveled at the big green arch door that led to such a tiny home.

"Oh, come in, come in, Timneet." Ne'Amin's mother pushed the dishes on the floor aside to open the door for Ne'Amin and Timneet.

"Hallo, Mama Birikhti." Timneet approached the woman, offering a kiss to each cheek and a third peck for respect's sake. Timneet bent down to the floor to help her clear the dishes from the entrance.

"Nonsense child, go on inside and help my boy with his studies. You've been doing fine work. Ne'Amin is happier going to school."

Timneet looked over at Ne'Amin who was grinning.

"Timneet, this is my mother's sister, Mama Helen." Ne'Amin pointed to a woman seated on a bench in their courtyard.

"Hallo, Mama Helen, how are you?"

"Thanks be to God, we are all fine, my child," Mama Helen replied. "You've got yourself a beautiful girl, Ne'Amin."

His cheeks grew flushed, before he excused himself to the other room. Timneet trailed behind as she said, "Pleasure meeting you, Mama Helen. Thank you for everything, Mama Birikhti. You are too kind."

Timneet followed Ne'Amin into his tiny bedroom where they lay their book on his bed, kneeling on the floor, bracing their knees with pillows beneath them.

"Let's start where Memhir Petros left off—," Timneet began.

Ne'Amin brought his hand to meet Timneet's outside hip, pulling her closer to him. He snuck kisses to her lips, while she watched the door for his mother and aunt.

Ne'Amin stopped suddenly to confess. "Timneet, do you know I would do anything for you?" he asked. "I think you're beautiful, and I've never seen anyone like you. You know the other boys tease me and say you're to be my wife one day." He returned his gaze back to his pencil, twirling it between his fingers. "I think someday you will be."

I wish it could happen. I wish there wasn't a war getting in the way of our lives. I wish I could say yes, it will happen someday, she thought. Instead, Timneet offered more uplifting words. "I would love for nothing more."

He grinned and nodded, as if to say, *It will happen.*

At the end of their mathematics assignment, it was time for Timneet to head home. Adey would be expecting her help with dinner. As he had done each time before, Ne'Amin walked Timneet the one-hour trail back to Zigib, as they professed their love for one another. Their time together soon came to an end when they reached Timneet's doorstep, and as Ne'Amin prepared to depart, he shared, "Before I forget, I have a surprise for you."

"Really?" Timneet knew her face was reddening. It only happened in Ne'Amin's presence.

"Yes, but I'll have to give it to you tomorrow."

"How come?" Timneet asked, pumping her fists on her hips. First Abo Solomon, and now, Ne'Amin—it seemed that everyone required Timneet's patience.

"My Timneet, the wait will only last for one day."

"Tomorrow it is, then." They had not had an argument yet, and Timneet was not interested in being the reason for one.

Ne'Amin quickly scanned Timneet's street, and when the road was clear of civilians, he rushed a peck to her lips. Timneet giggled as Ne'Amin scurried off.

She entered her home and jumped at the sound of whimpering from the kitchen. There Adey lay, mourning in the dark. The old woman sat between two candles, one lit for her son and the other for his wife, as she desperately cried, "Send them back to me, Lord." Timneet dropped her school bag on the floor and slowly paced her way to Adey.

"Send them, oh Lord, send them back please." Timneet matched the old woman's cries and together they sung their pleas to the heavens. Timneet cried not only for the parents who so lovingly raised her and taught her to be the soldier she already was, but she wept for her grandmother who would soon have no one to share tears with and no one to hush her to sleep at night.

The cries Timneet stirred within were far louder than those emitted from her mouth, as the ones she kept within tapped the depth of misery. For her grandmother, Timneet grieved, as the old woman outlived all but two grandchildren. For the old woman Timneet grieved, as she had never known the meaning of peace and would only be further from knowing peace when her only present grandchild would soon leave for an indefinite period of time. They hadn't heard from Amaniel since his departure, and although Timneet guessed he had joined the liberation effort, they did not know if he was alive or dead. For the old woman Timneet wept, and it was far too heavy a burden for her heart to carry. She kissed her grandmother on her aged cheeks and held her meek body close to hers. Timneet felt the lump in her throat grow larger with each plea her grandmother sang.

"*Melke my son, Melke my only son, Melke my poor son, Melke my son,*" she sang in agony for her beloved son to return home. Timneet listened with the ears of an orphan child, her eyes swelling at the sounds of her dear father's name. The weeping duo, grandmother and grandchild, sat in the middle of the cooking flour and spices that dusted the cement of their front yard for more than two months. Timneet and her grandmother had been borrowing food from their neighbors until the government approved rations for their home.

"*Rosa, my sweet daughter. Rosa, my dear daughter,*" the elderly woman continued. She followed with the name of the beloved wife of her son, pleading for her to grace them with her beauty again. Timneet joined her grandmother in singing for the return of her mother to take them out of their misery. They wept until the candles extinguished on their own.

"Let's go, Adey. Please, let me take you to bed." Timneet took her grandmother by the arms in the dark and led her to their cold cot inside the home.

The old woman whimpered in response. Adey continued to repeat the names of her late children.

Knowing that she would contribute to more of the old woman's pain sent pressure to Timneet's lungs.

Adey's cries were interrupted by several knocks at the door.

"Who could that be? Adey, are you expecting someone?" Adey didn't answer except to continue crying. Timneet shook her gently as she lay on the cot. "Adey, did you ask someone to visit you?"

The thumping came again, swifter and also lighter this time, almost like taps.

"It is probably your friend, child. She came looking for you ten times today. Go see what she wants."

"What did she say when you answered the door?" Timneet asked.

"She wouldn't say anything. She only said she needed you," Adey answered.

Timneet ran to the door.

"Are you alright, Miri?"

"Where were you?" She hurried in.

"I was with my love, Miri," Timneet crooned. She pulled Miriam by her hands, squealing, "He said he wants me to be his wife someday."

"Timneet, Abo Solomon came to my home."

"Is he postponing again? Miri, I'm not certain I believe—"

"Timneet," Miriam spoke above a whisper. "We're leaving," she added, "for coffee dipped in spice."

"What do you mean? When?"

"Midnight at the foot of the hill. Do you have your secret bag ready?"

"Midnight? In a few hours? Tonight?"

"Yes!" Miriam hissed.

"But Adey," Timneet thought of her weeping grandmother, "and Miri, Ne'Amin has a surprise he said he'd give me tomorrow—"

"Are you joking, Timneet? This was *your* idea!"

"I know but Miri, what about Adey? You see, she's still in mourning, and if I leave…what if she dies?"

"Timneet, I'm giving up my family, too. I am not here to force you. If you decide to stick to the vow we made two months ago in front of Tedros and Henok and the rest of our friends' bodies, then I'll be at the bottom of the hill at midnight." Miriam choked on her last few words, opening the door to leave.

Timneet tapped the back of her head against the door after closing it. *I could never break a vow*, she thought.

Timneet tiptoed into the bedroom. She climbed into bed and snuggled as close as she could to Adey, being careful not to awaken her. Timneet took note of details to last her for however long she was to be away. She breathed in Adey's scent, a mixture of turmeric and sweet flour, a sign that Adey spent her hours hard at work in the kitchen. Timneet pled with her memory to never forget the familiar, sweet aroma. She played with the loose ends of Adey's braided hair while she snored lightly, grumbling at times in between breaths. Timneet remembered how Adey had joked about cutting Timneet's hair if she failed in school, memories she wanted to retain forever.

Timneet caressed the old woman's skin and leaned over to softly kiss a few wrinkles on her back. With five minutes left until midnight, Timneet rose from the cot and gave her dear grandmother one last look. She carefully removed the bag of clothes hidden underneath the cot which her and Adey shared and walked out of the room, telling herself to only go forward. *Don't look back*, she repeated.

By midnight, Timneet had walked to the bottom of the hill dressed in her school clothes and met Miriam, who was dressed exactly the same. On the road of darkness during their walk to meet Abo Solomon, not one word, nor one sound was shared between Timneet and Miriam. Their eyes and teeth were the only source of light for one another, and in the black of the night, they firmly held hands and guided each other on a path they had taken since they were old enough to walk.

Soon enough Timneet and Miriam approached their assigned meeting place, the back alley of a welding shop. The girls awaited the sign, the bulb of the exterior light hanging from the roof to flash three times. Finally, the light flashed on and off, and Timneet fought the urge to look back as she and Miriam stepped out of the shadows and toward the shop. Timneet fought an even more overwhelming sensation to run back. As if Miriam read her thoughts, she let go of Timneet's hand and softly pinched Timneet on her elbow, whispering, "Be strong." Two words, fierce with encouragement, restored Timneet's faith in moving onward. There was no point in staying behind, of dreaming of a marriage to Ne'Amin and thinking she could save her grandmother from despair, when the regime would never give them peace.

There is no turning back now, she thought. As much as she wanted to take a final glimpse of the village behind her, albeit in its lightless state, she vowed to never look back at Zigib again.

The hours of the night were long. The three traveled north until the sun crept into the sky. The sounds of the night, the laughs of hyenas, the rustling of grass—often times Timneet lost sensation of the hand interlocked with Miriam's. Timneet kept her eyes on Abo Solomon who always walked several steps ahead. The full bearded man was quite tall, unusual for an elderly man. His hair and beard were almost completely gray. This worked in favor of the old man and the girls for the regime rarely stopped and questioned the elderly, even if they were accompanied by children.

After hours of walking and the noise of the surrounding land became too quiet, Timneet wondered aloud, "Abo Solomon, what do you do at your shop?"

"Abo Solomon, where is your family now?" Miriam followed.

"Do your kids attend school at Ger'hiwet or at Asgedmo, or are they fighting, too?" Timneet continued, hoping to hear his fatherly voice.

Abo Solomon put a halt to their curiosity. He was a man of few words, but when he did speak, it was low. "Only speak when you are spoken to, young ones. Do you understand me?"

This was no time for chatter or games. The girls had made a

decision to escape, and there was no room for child's play. Timneet was determined to listen to Abo Solomon, not because she valued obedience, but because she knew that a punishment coming from him had the potential to end their lives at the moment he saw fit, even though Miriam claimed he would never do such a thing.

The trio traveled only at night and dwelled in dark, hollow caves during the day. After four nights, Timneet and Miriam were delivered to the battle ground's training camp. As Abo Solomon prepared to return to Zigib, Timneet and Miriam outstretched their arms. It was time to bid farewell. The old man refused.

"Miriam, you and your friend here have to stay strong. No emotions out there." He pointed to the field in front of them. "Use this always," Abo Solomon tapped his head. "And this," he concluded his counsel by patting his heart, "never. Am I understood?"

In unison, Timneet and Miriam replied, "Yes, Abo Solomon."

A soldier approached them, the flag of the freedom fighters, the flag which was kept hidden in the villages, billowed and fluttered from the gun strapped across his back.

Abo Solomon placed one hand on the soldier's arm while shaking hands with the other. "Take care of these girls," he instructed. Abo Solomon turned his attention to Timneet. "This is Melke's daughter."

The soldier turned to Timneet. "She's in good hands, Abo."

How does he know my father? Timneet looked up at the old man who hadn't uttered a single word about her father until now. His stare was piercing, sending a cold spell throughout her body. She was not bold enough to ask the burning question. *There must be good reason for Abo Solomon to keep this from me,* Timneet reasoned.

Abo Solomon struck the ground with his cane once, gave the girls a military salute, and disappeared into the night.

CHAPTER 5

Narrated by Ma'arinet Neguse

And the day came when the risk to remain tight in a bud was more painful than the risk it took to blossom.
—Anaïs Nin

"…and Lord, in addition to blessing our meal, we know there are people 'round this world who won't receive food today, so we ask that you bless 'em with a kind soul to put food in front of 'em, or give 'em change enough for their next meal, or more. Last, we know our days are numbered Lord, so we ask that you keep us appreciative of the time we have left here on Earth…especially with one another." Reid whispered, "Amen."

Drea's grip tightened on my hand before letting go, and I was certain she had done the same with Reid. She adjusted her brunette wig.

"This one's got me itchin' a storm." Drea confessed in her southern accent. I watched her pat her head lightly.

"Why don't you take it off, honey?" Reid asked.

"Maybe when it's a little warmer. You know, these make for great hats," Drea replied, giggling.

"You're too adorable." Reid looked at Drea like a man madly in love with his soul's mate. He turned to me and asked, "Maari, did you want any water?"

"Sure, I'll take some. Thank you."

"Honey, special juice?" he asked his wife.

"Thank you, honey." Drea offered a forced smile. As Reid turned to leave for the kitchen, she looked over at me and stuck her tongue out in a gagging motion, like a child behind a parent's back when forced to eat Brussels sprouts.

It had been two years since our first assignment together, when Reid revealed Drea's battle with breast cancer. Just as Reid had predicted, Drea did survive, beating the disease with prayer and an unrelenting faith. In the last few months, though, she faced another attack on her body, this time on her ovaries. After meeting Drea for the first time during a study session with Reid in their home, only two strands of hair left on her head from weeks of chemotherapy and yet spewing all things positive, I knew we would be closer than sisters someday. Luckily, I was right.

Drea nibbled on her kale and quinoa salad as Reid clinked cups together in the kitchen. We sat on the carpeted floor in front of their fireplace, wrapped in Christmas themed blankets adorned with reindeer and snowflakes, our dishes lying close by on plush pillows. The logs crackled, at times like fireworks, as the flames turned them to ash. Snow sprinkled the city through the window of their one bedroom apartment along Lake Shore Drive, overlooking a slushy Lake Michigan. The colorful lights hanging from their white Christmas tree in the corner of the living room flickered on and off. The love and warmth in company such as theirs made me dread having to leave, like when my mother picked me up from Sarsum's on Sunday mornings after slumber parties when we were younger. Only *this* was more about avoiding the hellhole that had become my home.

"You know what I've learned, Maari?"

Yes, tell me all of it. Bless me with your wisdom, Drea. Reid and I no longer shared classes, but I still frequented their home. They never voiced it, but I always wondered if Reid and Drea knew that these visits were more like therapy sessions for me. Esak hurled me on a roller coaster ride since his mother's first phone call, begging him and his siblings to help her pay for an attorney. He shred me apart emotionally, then built me back up with plenty of *I'm sorrys* and *I'll never hurt yous*, only to tear me down again and again. Unwittingly, Drea and Reid infused my soul with the strength to make changes in my life, including considering leaving Esak. His hands had grown too wild for my skin's comfort.

"What is it, Drea?" I asked.

She leaned over, staring into the space above my head, and preached philosophy in such a way that made me wonder why I hadn't found her sooner in life. "I've learned that nothin' is more frightenin' than the realization you could be a prisoner in your own life."

I knew she meant the disease that confined her to hospitals and her home, but I too felt like a captive in my life, only my sickness was a man named Esak. Drea knew about my problems at home, and her ability to speak to my soul was breathtaking, including the conversations that touched my deepest sorrows. All of the name calling, the insults, the physical brawls in our home—Esak had made me feel as though beauty, love, and I were all strangers who would never have the fortune of meeting.

I left their apartment, carrying Drea's words like a garlic necklace, preparing to sling the extra cloves in my pocket at the first sight of fangs. I *always* prepared for the worst, and that is exactly what I got.

***

That night, I unlocked the front door and stepped foot inside the apartment like a thief in the night. I hiked my feet in the air and landed on my toes, hoping the sound of my footsteps wouldn't be met with Esak's pouncing. A stealthy entrance had become my ritual since the day I caught Esak sitting in the dark a couple of years ago, the day he first lay hands on me.

"Esak, you home?"

Our apartment was quiet. I turned on the light switch. He had left the house a complete mess, his underwear and bath towel steps from the front door.

"Really?" I muttered. I sat my purse on the barstool tucked in the corner of our kitchen and hung my key ring on the protruding nail above the gas stove. I went through each section of the apartment picking up his clothes from the ground.

"Esak?" After checking behind each screen and the bathroom, it seemed to be safe territory. I even checked under the bed to make certain. "Whew. Thank God," I said aloud.

I went back to the kitchen and checked the Caller ID on the counter. "NM Corrections," followed by his eldest brother, Ermias' phone number. Esak and Ermias had a closer relationship than their two sisters. Although neither of the four knew the genuine identities of their fathers, Esak and his brother, nearly six years apart, looked identical with stocky bodies fit for sumo wrestling and skin as light as butter. When I first spoke to Terar on the phone, she joked she would bet money on the fact that their *daddies* were the same man—by the sounds of it, she didn't even know. According to Esak, he and Ermias were convinced their fathers were white, not only because of their complexion, but because of the way Terar paraded about with white men in their living room when they were younger. The closest Esak had ever gotten to who *may* have been his and Ermias' father was a framed photograph of a man's coffin —no name, no background, just a coffin.

A preview of Esak's wrath came in the form of an imaginary storm-filled cloud above my head every time a call came in from Terar. I raised my face to the ceiling and prayed with open eyes. When I lowered my gaze, a fresh, gaping hole in the wall stared back at me.

"What in the world?" I whispered. I inched closer and placed my hands against the wall that had caved in. I patted the cracks surrounding the hole, like it was the face of a long lost love.

Damage and our home met quite often: the bathroom mirror, the closet door, the light fixture hanging in the hallway, my prized framed photos along our walls. If I knew Esak as well as I thought, he was surely roaming the streets in a destructive mood. My only job at that very moment was to get out while I still had the chance. I raced about the apartment like my life depended on it—only I feared it actually did.

Grab your toothbrush. I sprinted to the bathroom and resurfaced in the living room shortly after with my green toothbrush in hand. I stood there looking every which way for my next move.

Where'd I hide my emergency bag? The panic caused amnesia at times.

Closet! I yelled at myself. I grabbed hold of my bag and found it to be empty. *I didn't replace my clothes from before? What good is an overnight bag if it's not ready to go?*

I scurried around the bedroom screen and threw the first top and jeans in my reach into the bag. I snatched my camera bag, and no sooner than fastening its last buckle did my ears ring with the rattling of keys at the front door.

My stomach abandoned me, leaving a void so powerful I nearly collapsed to my knees. A lump formed in my throat and like a stuck piece of meat, I could neither swallow nor spit the bulge out. I was losing air.

I should've left my toothbrush. That bag should've been packed. It's my fault. It's all my fault.

I poked my head behind the screen on the side with the front door view. Wide-eyed, I attempted to predict what kind of trouble I would find myself in.

Esak stumbled in, made his way to the kitchen, and knocked down what I could only imagine was the spice rack onto the floor.

I brought my head back behind the screen and looked to the ceiling once again. *Take me out, Lord.*

"I don't care what she say." Esak slurred his words.

I remained silent, hoping his eyes were as blurred as his words, and that I'd become invisible. I scanned the bedroom, frantically searching for a place big enough to hide.

Should I jump in bed? Act like I'm sleeping?

"Maari! Maari!" Esak shouted, barely keeping his syllables together. "You stupid…," and the rest, the liquor was kind enough to soak.

Under the bed? I had tried to wrap myself with the covers underneath the bed a handful of times, and it worked, until the last time when Esak found me and dragged me out by my ankles. That was when the district attorney held a string of consecutive character bashing weeks against Terar and her *associates.* We learned in that same week Esak would be visiting her prison for the next thirty-two years if Terar lost the war in court, and I would deal with the violent aftermath in our home. It was an idea I was slowly, albeit silently, repelling. *No, beneath the bed won't work,* I reminded myself.

"Maari!"

Before I could think of anywhere else to hide, Esak kicked the bedroom screen door over. I stood there, crouched over the bed with the divider on my back.

"I would *never* do you wrong. They don't mean nothin' to me." Esak clumsily moved from the head of the bed to the foot, and paced back again, across from me, stretching out his arms and puckering his lips. Red lipstick stains decorated the bottom of his shirt.

"Okay, Esak," I whispered, "okay." I climbed from underneath the screen.

"I'm not playing, Maar. I can prove it. Watch," he snarled.

He rushed within inches of my face, grabbed hold of my wrist, and forced me to follow him out the front door.

"Esak, my shoes!" I shrieked, reaching for the floor before the door shut behind us.

"You don't need them," he barked.

I tiptoed on the tile floor as Esak pulled me through the glass double doors of our apartment building. It must have been five below outside and my bones felt every drop in temperature. With each step I took, it was like I was being thrown into a freezing pool with a base of needles. The wind struck my face and body, throwing me around like a rag doll, and the only stability I had was Esak's clenching grip, forcing me upright. My wrist and arm had gone numb from the squeezing, and soon, the frigid sidewalk had done the same to my bare feet.

"Stay here," he warned, jerking my hand down as he let go. Esak walked backwards while still facing me. I shook uncontrollably, more from fear than the cold.

He stumbled his way toward the dashed lines in the center of the road. I watched in horror as cars honked and swerved to avoid hitting him.

Esak sat on the street and lay flat, screaming like a mad man, "I *only* love Maari Neguse!"

I ran into the blinding oncoming headlights, waving my hands in opposite directions to catch the attention of cars coming from the north and the south.

"I would die for you, Maari!" he shouted while sobbing.

"Get up Esak!"

"Only if you promise you'll be here forever."

"Get out of the street!" a driver yelled from his car as he swerved around us.

Brakes screeched to a halt and horns honked wildly.

"What the hell is wrong with you?" shouted one driver.

"Somebody call the cops," yelled another.

"Promise me, darkie. Damn you're so dark." Esak slung what he liked to call, a *jokey insult.*

I ignored it like I had all the other things that over time had stomped my soul into the ground. I placed my chest against Esak's and used my upper body to try and pick him up under his arms. After several attempts and an angry crowd of vehicles threatening to run us over, honking and yelling out their windows, I yelled, "Someone help me, please. He's sick!" My heart was on the verge of stopping.

From the pick-up truck nearest Esak's body, a man with an afro that looked like it didn't want to be left behind in the 70s got out and strode toward us. He grabbed Esak under his arms and dragged him to the sidewalk.

"You're so stupid. You couldn't figure out how to do that by your-self?" Esak snarled at me.

"You alright, young lady?" The gentleman asked me, frowning and clearly disturbed by Esak's words.

"I will be. Thank you, sir."

"Alright, now. Y'all be safe."

With one of Esak's arms around my shoulder and him leaning on my side, we baby-stepped our way home, arriving a half an hour later when it normally would have taken us two minutes. We reached home and I put him to bed, walking to the living room to have a private conversation afterwards.

"I fulfilled my duty. I saved a man's life. Can I now have some peace in *my* life?" I asked the skies. It was a message that instead was stopped by the ceiling of our dark apartment.

"Man," Esak replied and the expletives began, only stopping when the drinks of the night finally disrupted the peace in his stomach and got the best of him. He rushed to the bathroom, nearly knocking both screens down to the floor.

"If that's your way of peace, then thank you." I spoke to the skies once more. *This is my chance*, I thought. I grabbed my emergency and camera bags I had thrown under the bed earlier, while Esak heaved in the bathroom. I wasted no time searching for a coat. I threw on the only shoes I could find, an unmatched pair, and darted from the apartment like a crook, running crazily, while the true thief, a robber of my joy and peace, remained free in our home.

The late night bus rides to my parents' were never easy.

"Good evening!" The same driver I had seen for the last week of late night escapes greeted me with a smile bright enough to make me mirror his mood—though mine was fake and temporary.

"Hi," I said.

I passed him and immediately oncoming tears stung my nose. I plopped down in my seat in the middle row of an empty bus and caught the bus driver's stare through the rearview mirror. It was a look of concern, a frown that reached his eyes. I was a mess, disheveled hair, wearing a house slipper on one foot and a two-inch wedged heel on the other.

I rubbed my wrist, throbbing from all the pulling and squeezing at Esak's hands.

I can't keep letting this happen to me.

***

One week passed before I gained the courage to call Sarsum and share my secret.

"I need you, Sar."

"What's going on?"

"I just need you to hurry over."

"Ok, I'll be there in an hour."

"No, he'll be back then."

"Who, Esak? Maari, did he hurt you again?"

"Sar, just hurry up."

Ten minutes later, a knock on the door eased my nerves. My very best friend walked in with a shower cap over her head and threw her keys on the kitchen counter. I knew I could count on Sarsum. She was willing to drop everything for me, including a hair treatment session.

"Did that foo' touch you again?" Sarsum scowled, pacing throughout the apartment.

"Sar, listen. Just sit down."

"Maari, you have to leave. There's no time for sitting and talking. This is *exactly* how it starts out. Don't you watch the news? First, the beatings, then they turn around and kill, all the while, family and friends are sitting around a coffin sayin', 'I had no idea he had even touched her.' I will *not* let that happen to you."

"Sar, sit down. That's why I called you over."

"What? Why?" Sarsum finally sat by my side.

"Sar, you can't tell a soul."

"You have my word." Sarsum folded her hands in her lap like an obedient child, eager to receive.

"I'm serious, especially not to your mother."

Sarsum's mother was a woman dangerously equipped with the secrets inside everyone's home in the Midtown area, serving coffee to her friends and sharing her latest piece of news.

"Scout's honor." Sarsum lifted her two fingers. Our mothers never let us join the Girl Scouts for fear that we'd be snatched while selling cookies door to door. Since Sarsum and I weren't allowed to join all of our friends, we initiated ourselves into a secret society of our own, forming promise codes only shared between us, like the rise of the index and pinky fingers instead of the first three fingers. Our secret code carried on into adulthood.

"Maar, will you get it out already?"

I sighed. It was the first time I would ever utter the words that had been haunting my mind day in and day out. "I'm leaving."

I watched Sarsum look at me as though I had told her I won the lottery and was giving her half of the lump sum. "Hallelujah! Praise Jesus!" Sarsum exclaimed, squirming on the futon beside me.

"Listen, I need you to help me." I tapped Sarsum's hand, urging her to be more serious.

"Anything!" Sarsum had been trying to get me to leave since the first day I told her of Esak's temper. I was certain she was relieved to hear that I had reached my breaking point.

"I'm going to take my belongings over to your house little by little until I break the news to my mom and dad." *My mom and dad*, my voice echoed in my head. *This is going to break their precious hearts.*

My parents only agreed to my moving in with Esak for two reasons. First and foremost, he was Eritrean and to my parents, this meant we would have whole Eritrean children to whom we could pass on the traditions and cultures of our people. We purposely neglected to tell them we only were certain of half his heritage, Terar's side, and we didn't speak much of Terar either. Secondly, Esak convinced both my mother and father he would take care of me as he would want a man to take care of his daughter when the time came. I wished he hadn't lied.

"Maari, whatever you need I'm here." She held my hand. "But, I don't want you to wait for long. Why don't you just leave now? What's stopping you?"

"I have to wait until his double shift on Friday. It's the only full day I'll have of moving. I've already asked Reid to help me. Hey Sar...," I hesitated to continue.

"Yeah?"

"There's another reason why I'm waiting until Friday," I began. I trusted my best friend, and I knew if ever there were a right time to tell her about the biggest change in my life, it was then.

"I have a shipment coming in on Friday morning." I lowered my head, not sure of how to break the news.

"Yeah? What for?" Sarsum asked, not paying me any mind as she was more intrigued with stuffing a small suitcase with clothes. We had moved into the bedroom.

"Well," I paused before stretching the rest of my words, "I ordered a crib." I had placed the order over a month ago, well before my decision to leave. Luckily it was coming on a day when Esak wouldn't be home and I could take it with me along with my other belongings.

"A cr—? What!"

A number of knocks banged on the front door, making us both jump.

"Who is it?" I asked, approaching the door.

"Maari, it's me."

"Ees?"

"I forgot my house keys."

"Okay, hang on," I yelled, hurrying back to Sarsum in the bedroom. "Listen, I'm giving you these to borrow, and you don't know *anything* about the baby, okay?"

Sarsum nodded her head, vigorously. She talked a whole lot, but when it came to facing Esak, she seemed just as, if not more, terrified than me.

"Hey Ees, I just came over to borrow some clothes, nothing else. Nothing at all."

I looked at Sarsum in disbelief. *You might as well just tell him the truth*, I thought.

"Guys, I have to get going. You know how strict my mom is."

"Yeah, you do that," I answered, frustrated with Sarsum for not pulling her Oscar-winning moves like she had done the first time she met Reid when she told him she was driving me home.

The door closed shut behind Sarsum, and Esak began with his suspicions.

"So, what were you and Sarsum talking about?"

"Nothing, she came by to borrow some clothes."

"Did you tell her you were pregnant again?"

"No, I didn't."

"Good. I don't want her mother running her mouth like she did when we lost the first baby."

"I know, I know."

"And calm all that eatin' down. I can't have you blowin' up this early in."

I put the slice of apple back down on the fruit tray and urged myself to remember. *Only four more days. Friday will be here before I blink again. Ajoki*, I reassured myself, *everything will be alright.*

Esak left the room to shower.

"You're my saving grace." I stroked my belly and stuffed my face with six slices of apple.

***

It was finally Thursday, and Esak had no clue I was leaving the next day. If he had, he surely didn't show me a sign. He was his normal self, belligerent and heartless.

"You're too good to open your eyes?" he asked, hanging from the side of the bed. I lay on the floor. I could no longer stomach sleeping by his side. I kept my eyes shut, hoping the swallowing sands from my nightmare would have me again. His breath smelled like whiskey, his top choice for poison. I shifted my head farther from his stench.

No, I just don't want to see your face. Or mine, I thought.

"So, blind and deaf. Is that the game we're playing today? I'm talking to you, Maari." His feet made a thud onto the ground. I flung my eyes open for the first time, staring directly above at the black blotch of a dead spider. Squinting made it easier to block Esak from the corner of my eye, and it put me more at ease.

Esak lunged over my body one hefty limb at a time, like I was cow dung in the middle of the bedroom. Lying on my back, I hugged my only companion of the night, an open bible on my chest. I cringed. I had become weak, something my mother taught me to avoid at all costs. He had extinguished any trace of strength. I no longer recognized myself.

He turned around, crouched down, and sent another gust of liquor. "Forget you."

Esak *loved* to forget me. Within a matter of two weeks, he lost his memory of how I had saved him from oncoming traffic while he professed his drunken love.

I fell into a trap, one I set myself. Somewhere down the line, I made the mistake of believing I could teach Esak how to love. *If* was my favorite word. *If* I love him more, *if* I save him, *if* I teach him while remaining patient…then it would all get better, or so I believed. The word *if* was going to be the death of me. I made excuses time and time again, thinking Esak would spare me from clashes with the walls and calling me nasty names, ones that you wouldn't repeat in front of children.

"Maari!" he yelled in my ear.

Please God, not today. Please let him rest his sharp words, his angry hands, and temper. Let his heart function today and resemble that of a caring human being. Can You make it beat and properly circulate his blood, so that he isn't so harrowingly cold? I need his heart to feel today. Just for today, God, just for today. I mumbled the prayer, but I assured God that although it was rushed, I meant every single word.

"You have got to be one of the most selfish people I know. You want all the attention in the world, don't you? You like all this sympathy stuff. You…," and the rest, Esak's tongue was kind enough to retire. His method of refraining from certain word choices did not come often. It must have been an intervention of the divine. Despite Esak's decision not to continue on his rant, I still had feelings, and his words still stung.

I covered my child with a pillow and folded my hands underneath—my fingers were becoming numb and were probably losing all color from the tight grip I refused to release. I tweaked the prayer. I figured God was a tad bit busy with a torched village amidst a civil war in some remote part of the world, a single mother on her last dime with no food for her children, or other helpless human beings far greater in peril than I. I thought I should ask for a favor a little less challenging.

Ok, Lord, how about you just numb me and make me deaf—temporarily, just until he leaves for the day. Or, maybe just until the cycle turns in my favor—he comes home from work, gets on his knees, and apologizes. I'll do anything You ask of me. Just for today Lord, numb and deaf. Take them both, for a number of hours, until all is normal again. Our normal, that is.

"What in the world is wrong with you? You hear me talking to you?" He rose from beside me and picked up the nearest object within reach of his fingertips, a hammer on the study desk. The tool was part of a heavy duty kit I had bought him last Christmas. Esak stepped behind the screen and I watched his shadow pace. I could tell he was trying to talk himself out of using the hammer…on me.

"Esak, put the hammer down," I urged from the floor on the other side of the screen. *What did I ever do to deserve any of this? I've given you so much of me.*

"Esak…," I whispered. I could tell the alcohol hadn't left his system. He raised his arm over his head and hurled the hammer through the paper screen door. I put my hands in the air, forward of my face. It was a protective mechanism I had grown accustomed to using, an acquired movement as vital as blinking and as habitual as dreaming.

I shrieked and gave him the frightful response that seemed to calm him, almost as though it made him happy.

Take me, whole! I don't care how you do it, just take me out of my misery. I beg of You, God, take me now.

In the middle of my one-sided conversation with God as if Esak felt His wrath, he walked toward the kitchen without saying another word.

Why won't You take me? I'm not wanted here. I want to be with You. Make my heart stop—it just needs one final clout. You can make me bleed to death right here on this floor. Or, You can come down and save me Yourself. Esak doesn't fear You, otherwise he would respect and love me as Your child, but maybe, just maybe, if You came down and saved me Yourself, maybe he would transform into the respectable, loyal, compassionate, trustworthy, and above all, You-fearing man I had hoped time would turn him into.

I closed my eyes and held my cries, heightening my hearing. I listened for the pattern of his footsteps on the kitchen's hardwood floors. Over the years, I learned to anticipate Esak's next move, which gave me several seconds to prepare my own. I didn't have many options. It was either grab a shield, recollect my self-defense moves, ones I learned in a course I had taken for the purpose of what I liked to call *domestic defense*, or think of words that weighed heavy enough to sway his state of mind. On occasion, pacing was good. It meant Esak was thinking. If his pacing came to an abrupt halt, followed by quick steps, I knew his next stop would be inches from my face. If his pacing was followed by slow, treading footsteps, I was safe—as safe as I could be.

A pain from deep within my stomach, followed by nausea, forced me to rise from the floor and make a run for the bathroom. I shut the door behind me and darted for the toilet. With my arms around the rim of its bowl, I fought the urge to expel what I could only imagine was either water or air, since I hadn't eaten in twenty-four hours.

I heaved. The little strength left in me was being used to hold on to the bowl.

God, why would You let this happen to me? He won't even check on me. I'm not even worthy of an, Are you ok? I'm not worthy of sticking his head through the bathroom door and seeing if I need anything? He has no sense of remorse, no heart. Am I not worthy?

I felt trapped, stuck. I was caged in, with prison bars made up of his incessant negativity, acidic words, and violent rampages. I continued to heave.

He barged through the bathroom door and marched back and forth behind me. "You're doing this to yourself. You make yourself sick. I have never in my life done you wrong. You drive yourself crazy and stress yourself out. If it weren't for you being so insecure, we wouldn't have to go through this. Over and over, you ask me the dumbest questions. Why do you do this to yourself?"

He's talking to himself, and I'm the one who's crazy? At least I think to myself and don't answer my own questions aloud. Is he trying to convince himself of his innocence, clear his conscience a little? Am I supposed to chime in, mid-heave, and assure him that he's right? That I am to blame for this, too? Or, it's possible he thinks I'm on the verge of dying, and if it actually happens, maybe he thinks he would be held responsible, given all the mess he's put me through. What is that called again… manslaughter?

"You're crazy, Maari. You're crazy." He slammed both of his fists into the door, one at a time, like he was up for a boxing match. Esak turned to me and I to him at the same time. I threw my hands in the air. He held his head in his hands, eyes to the floor. I swore he was on the brink of insanity. Either that or he was figuring out ways to take my life. He was good at that—taking.

I didn't recognize it before, but that's exactly what this is on his face, in his eyes—it's fear. The same fear he instills in me with the raising of his hand or the reaching for an object that has no value to him. Isn't that something? Could he possibly be feeling what I'm feeling?

"You're not right in the head. Why are you putting us through this?" Esak yelled with the pitch and tone of a two-year-old in a grocery store, screaming to make an audience out of surrounding shoppers.

A sharp, twisting pain met the right side of my belly like a knife, digging deeper with each breath. I doubled over, shrieking.

"Really? You want to play the victim?" Esak dashed to my side and kicked me in my back, twice. A gust of air escaped my mouth and sent me into a coughing fit, my eyes bulging. My body trembled as I gasped for more air. As if a switch had turned off in his brain, Esak heaved a sigh and said, "Let me know when you're done. I need to shave before I go to work."

I hadn't even regained control of my breath, and he was concerned with shaving. And, just like that, it was over. I turned on my back, at the foot of the toilet, holding onto my side and back with each hand. The pain had subsided, but my heart was still torn and bleeding heavily. I wiped my bottom lip with the back of my hand like I was cleaning blood after a punch to the jaw. *I must be crazy, staying with you for this long*, I thought.

I turned to my side and lifted myself up from the floor with my hands. Esak and I passed each other in the bathroom doorway without a word to exchange. I crawled into bed while Esak showered and prepared for work like it was any other day. Before long, the front door slammed shut. My brain hesitated, struggling to decide between hyperventilation and crying. I opted for both, wishing that in the midst of it all, my heart would retire. Somewhere between deep inhalation of panic and exhalation of sorrow,

I prayed my body would get caught in a simultaneous lock, and just give out. After nearly two years of volatile mornings like this one, I pled for it to happen sooner than later. And then I remembered, I had someone else to live for.

I caressed my stomach. "We're almost gone, my baby."

***

"Clean yourself up."

Esak's voice snapped me back into reality. I woke up to my hands and legs striking the floor like I was vying for gold in the longest race of my life. I would have much preferred being sucked alive by the quicksand in my terrifying dream than hear Esak's voice. They were recurring horrors that haunted my nights, yet still, I yearned for them. They took me away from Esak for hours at a time and offered me an escape that left me, during the day, begging for nightfall to come sooner. But, I wouldn't have to worry about that anymore. It was Friday. I ignored him. *Today is the day. Freedom,* I reassured myself.

"Wake up and clean yourself," he repeated. "And congratulations, Maari," I heard his footsteps move farther away as he applauded, "you managed to do it again." The front door banged shut shortly after. Esak was on his way to work his double shift and I was closer to freedom. Reid and Sarsum would be over in a few hours, the crib would arrive, and Esak would be out of my life forever.

I stretched before opening my eyes, moving my arms and legs about. A draft snuck through the sheets and a coolness reached between my legs. The sheets beneath me were damp.

Something isn't right. Why am I wet?

My eyes never left the ceiling. My palms met my bottom, patting and looking for answers. *That's too thick to be urine*, I thought. As the realization of what it might be settled, the room started to spin. "Please God, don't do this to me." I spoke softly, under my breath, almost bracing my lungs for screams. "No, no, not again. God, you wouldn't do this to me again!" I screeched. I needed to make sense of Esak's words and the sensation beneath me. I lifted my head and shoulders, taking a deep breath before I opened my eyes. And, when I did, the color red flashed before me.

"No, no, no, no, no, no , no…" I sang in pain.

I *sang* in pain.

I lost all feeling in my shoulders, and my head fell back to the ground. The *no's* escaping my mouth seemed endless. Each breath that left, I wanted to be my last. I stifled my cries, hiding my mouth in the crease of my arm, securing my elbow with the crease of my other arm. I would have used my palms, but they were painted in blood. They were painted in my child's blood.

"Oh my *God*."

"Oh my *God*."

"Oh my *God*."

The longer I stretched each vowel, the deeper the dagger went, my voice quivering throughout. My pitch was higher than I had ever heard. The tears filled my ears, and made me deaf to the world, including my own cries.

A pit replaced my stomach. I clenched the stained sheets in my fists, lifted my rear, and pulled them from underneath me. Dark red in color, I retched at the sight of my child's blood that soiled the sheets. My palms were stained with remnants of what would have been and there was absolutely nothing I could do to reverse the clocks and save her or him. My shorts, my shirt, the sheets, my palms—I was drenched in *it*, smelled like *it*, disgusted by *it*, and yet *it* was once a part of me.

It was to whom I sang the alphabet and lullabies.

It was supposed to be my savior.

It was my friend, my closest, when I could turn to no other.
It was to whom I promised the world.
It was who promised the world to me.

I crawled into bed, wrapped myself in the sheets from the floor, in the coolness of my own blood. A doctor wasn't needed. I had been through this once before, the only other time Esak robbed me of my future, when he had slapped me around for eight straight days before I lost our first child. My only remedy was being left in solitude to weep.

When and where did it all go wrong? What happened to me? They were questions with which I struggled every day.

I never prepared for the day my world would come to a screeching halt. For the past three months, I had been too occupied with selecting the right crib, purchasing bibs and pacifiers, and assuring myself that I could be a great single mother if I one day chose to leave. I had told myself that every day since I learned I was pregnant again. What I hadn't planned was that my baby would leave me before I got the chance to leave Esak.

It had been a few hours since Esak left for his double shift. By 10AM, my eyes were swollen and as red as my stained sheets. My fingers trembled the entire time as I cleaned the blood that seeped onto the tiles. I had become somewhat of a professional since my first miscarriage, swiftly cleaning my bed and apartment half an hour before my parents came to visit me and managing to keep my composure. They hadn't suspected a thing.

Here I am having to go through it again. At least I have more time to hide everything, including my feelings before Sar and Reid come.

I had just returned from the dumpster outside the apartment complex where I had thrown away the plastic bag filled with my shorts and bedding, knowing that Reid and Sarsum would arrive by 11AM. Reid and his father arrived right on time. They pulled up in Reid's bright red Jeep Wrangler and a rented pick-up truck. Reid's jeep was decorated with ribbons and a sign which I couldn't read from the bedroom window.

"Drea's idea," Reid said as he walked in the door, his father smoking a cigarette outside. She wanted you to know that she's here in spirit and wishes she could join in," Reid seemed to be searching his memory for Drea's exact words, "the celebration of a new you. She told me to tell you, 'Your journey's just begun.'"

"Wow, you've got an angel on your hands." I surrendered to my tears and sobbed openly.

"I know leaving is hard," Reid responded, giving me a hug.

"Reid, I lost my baby." There was a melt-down within my body that I wasn't sure how to cure. My eyes burned like my face had been shoved onto a stove. The walls were closing in on me and my lungs threatened a collapse that I didn't have control over. It was the first time I had uttered the words aloud since I saw the blood on my sheets and the suffocation that ensued was unreal.

"Oh my God, Maari," he held me tighter. "I'm so sorry!" Reid swayed me in his arms.

"I just want to get out of here. Please, let's do this as fast as we can," I pled.

"Listen, Maari," he pulled me away from his chest, grabbing me by the arms and lowering his head to my eye level, "why don't you stay with me and Drea for a little bit?"

I shook my head and wiped my tears with my shirt. "Thank you, but I-I need to go home."

"I understand," he said, pulling me in for another hug.

An older gentleman walked into the apartment smelling like cigarettes.

"Maari, this is my dad."

"Hi, how are you?" I extended my hand, sniffling.

"Washington Stone." Reid's father took a moment and looked closer at my face. "Are you alright young lady?" Mr. Stone asked, sporting a pistol on his belt.

"Yes sir, I'll be fine, thank you."

"What can I help with?" he asked.

"It's just boxes really. I've already got a couple of them packed with clothes in the bedroom."

I showed Mr. Stone the way. When he left the apartment to put the first box on the truck, I asked Reid, "What's with the gun?"

"You remember when you told me I was in luck when I asked you if you knew where my classroom was the day we first met?"

I nodded, not correlating what Mr. Stone's gun had to do with our photography class.

"Well, this time, *you're* in luck. My dad's a sheriff." He grinned. "That foo' comes back here startin' trouble, my dad will scare the bejesus out of him." He chuckled with his hands on his hips.

"*Uhhh*, I'm so grateful for you." I gave Reid another hug, overwhelmed by his and Drea's support.

For the next hour I packed my essentials while Reid and Mr. Stone lugged boxes into their vehicles parked outside our complex. I broke out the flattened boxes I had hidden under the bed and stuffed them with more clothes.

"What about this entertainment set? Are we taking it apart and moving it, too," Mr. Stone asked me and Reid.

"He can have it," I said.

"The bed?"

"He can have it."

"How about you tell us what you *want* to take?" Reid asked, smiling.

"Only boxes. I don't want a thing to remind me of him."

"Okay, boxes it is," Reid replied as he put his arm around my shoulder. "You alright, kiddo?"

"I will be," I answered. Although I was fearful of the unknown, my confidence lay in a brighter future. After all, nothing could be worse than the hell I had been living in.

As I continued to pack, I found an Eritrean flag belonging to Esak tucked at the bottom of the dresser drawer. It was the flag of the freedom fighters, those who were still in determined combat against Ethiopia.

For someone who was of mixed heritage, according to him, and raised by a white family, Esak sure did shout a love for Eritrea louder than most who were wholly Eritrean—but as most considered his cry to be one of loyalty, no one truly knew Esak's reality better than I. Esak shouted, *Eritrea!* and spoke of his blood incessantly but had frequent one night stands with Eritrea's daughters, breaking the spirit of one in particular—me. He shouted, *Eritrea!* to the world while he spewed hate and frequently made me weep into the night. Esak shouted, *Eritrea!* to the public, while he kicked me down behind closed doors, making me believe I was not worthy of love nor affection. Esak shouted, *Eritrea!* to his friends, while he tainted my soul, causing a pain no human being should ever feel. Esak shouted, *Eritrea!* and those who *knew* him, praised him for loving me, for loving Eritrea. They would *never* know his truth.

"Maari," Sarsum interrupted my trance. "You've got a long way to go, huh?" she asked, scanning the apartment that looked untouched.

"Hey love," I replied.

Sarsum's hand clasped the side of my hip closer to hers. "You doin' alright?" she asked, a nurturing mother's tone in her voice.

"Sar," I broke out in a cry, my emotions uncontrollable. "I lost it," I wailed, gripping my stomach.

"Lost wha—? Maari, no," Sarsum joined my cries. "What are you saying?" she whispered. We stood there for a few minutes in each other's arms as I tried my very best to cry the pain out of me.

I reached a point where I coughed so hard, Sarsum forced me to have a seat on the living room futon. She lay my head on her chest and patted my back, rocking my body to calmness.

Several minutes of silence passed as Sarsum rocked me to a quieter, more peaceful state. It had seemed like hours had gone by before Reid walked in with outstretched arms.

"Well, is that it, Maar?" he asked.

"That's all of it," I muttered. I sat up straight and confirmed with a final nod.

"Alright, well let's get goin' then. We don't wanna run into the guy."

"Ok, guys do you mind giving me a quick second. I'll meet you outside?" I asked my friends.

"Sure," Reid and Sarsum agreed at the same time.

"You're doing the right thing, Maari. Don't you ever forget that," Sarsum whispered in my ear. "I'm with you all the way."

"I won't forget, Sar." Her kiss was warm on my cheek. "I'll never forget," I told her.

They shut the door behind them, and I sat there for a moment, my heart still throbbing. *All this time I waited—and it was for nothing? I waited for a stupid crib and you were dying with each slap, every kick, and all the nasty words he fed me—you felt that too, didn't you? I fed you poison by staying here with him, didn't I? Had I left sooner, would you still be here?* I spoke to my empty womb as my eyes stung.

I grabbed my camera and letter from the coffee table and talked myself into going to the bathroom where I had a mission to complete before leaving Esak. Once I arrived, I faced the cracked mirror, a place I had bawled in front of on countless occasions. I taped my goodbye letter on the mirror. It was a note I had written just days before, in anticipation of Friday.

January 25, 1991

You built my pedestal with your lies, wooden and unstable. You took my hand and helped me as I climbed to the very top, until I was so high that I let your hand go to keep my balance. When I reached the top and you knew you had me exactly where you wanted, at my highest point, you took a flame and burned each of its legs, one by one, as I helplessly watched in horror. I was in too much shock and too high in the air to jump off and run. It crumbled to the ground, taking me with it. You saw me lying there on the ground, hurt, and you didn't even lend me a helping hand. Instead, you kicked me, right in my chest. As I took a deep inhale, gasping for air, I watched you kneel by my side and heard you whisper in my ear that I was no better than the heap of ash piled next to me that once was my pedestal. You convinced me that without you there wasn't the slightest chance of a living me. You were only able to succeed in making me feel this way because I let you.

And, I was the one who let you.

But, today? Today is my day. Soon enough, I'll laugh while you cry. I'll be in the presence of true love while you continue to struggle with lust and loneliness, one night at a time. I'll trust again while you continue to sow your lies. I'll be free while you're imprisoned by every haunting thought of what you've ever done to me. And, at the end of it all, I'll recognize the wrong in desiring all of this. I'll find it in my heart to forgive you while you will never be able to forget me. May God have mercy on your daughter's heart.

I lifted my camera from my neck and took a photo of my note to Esak, the serenity of a near liberation was pouring into me.

Click.

"*This* is the look of freedom."

CHAPTER 6

But responsibility hardens the heart. It must.
—Ford Madox Ford

"Your father was a great man." The freedom fighter did not smile. Instead, he looked to the distance as if in deep thought. Timneet mimicked his stares, only her thoughts were riddled with regret.

Abo Solomon said nothing about my father until he mentioned it to this man. I could've asked for more—for stories and good memories to fill the ones that leave me each day. Timneet looked down the dusty trail upon which she, Miriam, and Abo Solomon had walked. But though it had only been a few minutes, Abo Solomon had already disappeared into the night.

"My name is Mussie." He shook Timneet's hand first. It was a firm handshake. Timneet raised her head. Mussie was just as tall if not taller than Abo Solomon. He wore an afro, beard full and dark, and his shorts, tight and high on his legs.

He shook Miriam's hand next. "Abo Solomon brought you here because he knew you would be in good hands. You girls have made the best decision for your country."

"I didn't know he knew my father," Timneet muttered.

"We all did," Mussie shared. "He was a great part of the movement. Before they robbed us of your father, he and Abo Solomon were responsible for sending people our way. He treated everyone like his own son or daughter. I should know." Mussie placed his hand on his chest. "Melke brought me here years ago."

"*My* father brought *you* here?" Timneet asked.

"Yes, he did."

Mussie guided the girls forward with one hand on each of their backs. He walked with a puffed chest and legs that seemed rigid but mighty with the pounding of each foot on the ground. In the darkness of the night, Mussie led Timneet and Miriam to an open, desert-like field. When they reached the middle of emptiness, surrounded by a circle of stout trees, Mussie bent his knees, resting his seat on his ankles as he parted two sets of tied branches on the ground, exposing a hole just large enough for their bodies.

"Go on," he urged, jutting his chin toward the jagged, ripple-like steps flickering with light that shone from the bottom of the cave.

Timneet lay her feet carefully down each step, the cold beneath her thin sandals sending shivers to her skin. When she arrived at the bottom, her mouth became heavy, dropping—it was like the ants that formed colonies on her front doorstep back home. Freedom fighters in pairs and small groups decorated the inside of the cave as they marched along to plans of action and declarations of victory shouted among them. Timneet's ears caught snippets of conversation as they walked by them, capturing as much of the excitement as she could.

"We should take hold of…"

"Force them to their knees…"

"They caught seven yesterday and killed…"

"Take this lantern…"

"I hope it rains…we need…"

"The food came in yesterday and more is due…"

"We're lucky, others are fighting with low gun supply and…"

"We must destroy…"

"Viva Eritrea!"

Who would have known that the grounds above would look and sound like this below? Timneet thought.

Timneet felt Miriam breathing on her neck. They stood in silence and only moved when Mussie pushed them farther inside toward a group of attentive freedom fighters on the floor and a man with a deep, rumbling voice who stood before them.

As they grew nearer, Timneet realized that in the midst of the busy colony, a class was in session. It was just like school, only instead of logs, these students sat on the ground behind a teacher writing on and pointing toward one of the large slabs that made up the inside of the cave, and instead of students of English, these were students of war.

"They have hit our zones in Senait and Sahel. We must be strong in numbers in these areas. Collaborations are in progress with our brothers and sisters in Keren, Barka, and other areas."

Barka? Did he just say Barka? That's Ne'Amin's region. Timneet turned to Miriam who made no expression that suggested she had remembered Ne'Amin's origins.

"Now, you've all been given your weapons. You sleep with this by your side each night, not alongside one another…but with *these.*" The freedom fighter thrust his assault rifle in the air, his eyes danced wildly among the group of fifteen. "This is your closest comrade. It will save your life time and time again."

They are new like us. Timneet scanned the backs of her comrades.

"Berhane," Mussie called from behind, interrupting the teacher. "You have two nationalists here who would like close friends of their own."

"Very well, Genet, give the girls their weapons. And get them food, as well." Berhane pointed to a gaunt woman who raised a lantern in the air, leaving a few on the ground. Genet bowed her head quickly, twice, and closed her open hand as though she were catching a fly. Timneet recognized the gesture, as her mother used it to signal her closer in the very same way. As the girls approached Genet, Timneet heard Mussie behind her, "Yes...Melke." She turned around. Mussie was leaned in close to Berhane, gawking at her as she walked away with Miriam and Genet.

She walked rapidly behind Miriam to keep up with Genet as she was the only source of light. Still, Timneet tripped over the uneven earth beneath her feet multiple times. Cold drops of water met her head from the top of the cave, which grew more winding and narrow. Timneet cringed, jumping at the sight of rodents running fiercely along their feet. Her long sleeves and dress no longer kept her warm nor safe as they had on even the coldest nights while walking with Abo Solomon—the cave was frigid, her blood was turning cold, and her skin was become nibbling grounds for insects.

"Did one of you know Melke?" Genet asked as she stopped them before a section of protruding rock. "Did I hear correctly?" Mussie wasn't just loud enough for Timneet's ears.

"How does everyone know Abo Melke?" Miriam asked Timneet.

"Well, how did *you* know him?" Genet asked, smiling.

"He was my father," Timneet replied.

"Oh," Genet lowered her head. "I am sorry for your loss. We miss him."

Her face remained stripped of emotion, and Timneet recalled Abo Solomon's words to her and Miriam about not using their hearts here. Genet reached between overhanging pieces of rock with one hand and pulled two weapons. She handed them to Timneet and Miriam and said, "Do not let these leave your side, or else whoever finds it may force you to leave our side. Have you eaten?" Genet asked.

Timneet shook her head. It had been at least two days since their last meal with Abo Solomon.

Genet brought the girls deeper into the cave. She fixed small bowls of porridge. "You will never eat alone again. When there is food, we eat with one another right here, always." Genet pointed to the ground.

As she handed Timneet her meal, loud voices—men yelling far different cries than *Viva Eritrea*—echoed from the opening of the cave. Timneet and Miriam jumped, startled. Genet dropped the ladle, taking her weapon by its sash and bringing it between her side and her arm, her finger on the trigger. She moved swiftly toward the entrance of the cave with a lantern in her other hand paving the way to the front. Timneet whisked her head toward Miriam. Together, they rapidly lowered their bowls to the ground, grabbing hold of their new closest friends, and darted behind Genet. Timneet's feet shook as they struck the ground.

I don't even know how to use it. Please don't make me use it, she thought.

Timneet's fingers wrapped tightly around the weapon as she prayed that she would keep from shooting herself by accident, or worse strike Miriam ahead of her. She twirled her weapon to the ground, keeping its muzzle as far from her face and best friend as possible, holding it off to her side and by its handle instead. Each time her gun slipped between her hands, her heart skipped beats until she caught a better grip again.

"Move out of the way," a grizzled soldier growled. When they arrived, Genet relaxed, her shoulders sinking. They were not in danger. Timneet climbed to the balls of her feet. The freedom fighter behind the voice was followed by a string of others, all of them struggling under the weight of their wounded brothers and sisters on their backs.

Timneet stumbled backwards as the freedom fighters pushed

their way inside. The assault rifle strapped to the backs of some collided with the rocky wall behind them, clinking loudly. Genet regained her footing, dropped her weapon to the floor, and pushed her way through the crowd, offering her hands as she assisted each freedom fighter into refuge standing beside Mussie who was the first at the steps of the cave. "To your right. One more step," Mussie and Genet advised.

Mussie took the elbow of another freedom fighter, this one carrying an injured man who groaned, "I can't feel my foot. Is it there, brother? Answer me please, why can't I move it?"

The soldier carrying him did not respond, too focused on the hops and sidesteps necessary to avoid tumbling, which resulted in cries from the wounded man hanging from his shoulders.

"Ease this pain, Lord, please. Do not forsake me," another soldier moaned.

"Brother, where are we?" a third freedom fighter asked, shaking his head wildly.

"Lay them here on the ground," Mussie ordered. He hunched his back while walking, cautious of the jutting stones. Mussie investigated each case, walking with his hands clasped behind his back. "Move faster brothers and sisters. Water, gauze, rope," Mussie barked the urgent necessities.

Of the six freedom fighters dangling on the backs of others, four of them made sounds, while the other two, both women, remained still and quiet—one with a missing arm, and the other left with no legs, the latter sending Genet into a wild cry. Timneet shook her head and adjusted her pants. The cloth stuffed between her legs was soaked, threatening drops of blood down her thighs. *I am one of them. My sisters,* she sympathized, feeling Genet's pain.

Timneet and Miriam walked backward, lowering their weapons to the ground at the back wall near the entrance, and clasped hands with one another instead.

"I don't know what to do," Timneet whispered, as the students who looked her age ran at the chance to ask how they could be of service. They received their assignments from Mussie and Berhane and scurried off.

"Should we ask someone?" Miriam hesitated.

"Do you think we would be in the way?" Timneet asked.

"Girls!" Genet cried as she knelt by the side of a body laying still. "Hurry, get more water and gauze behind the pot where I gave you food." Her voice trembled, tears streaming down her face.

Timneet and Miriam stood frozen, watching Genet transform from a helpful, smiling yet fearless soldier to a blubbering child.

Genet returned to the woman on the ground, "Is this what you do? You leave me like *this*?" She placed her head on the woman's bloody chest. Luwamay!" Genet's screams halted the activity in the cave, forcing a moment of silence among the freedom fighters within earshot. A group of four brothers and sisters surrounded Genet and the lifeless woman. Genet wailed, "No!" as she beat her fists against the legless woman's chest, until Berhane rushed forward. He raised Genet from the ground by her waist and carried her farther into the cave. "Luwamay," Genet continued to weep, reaching her arms for the slain soldier.

"Who do you think that was?" Miriam whispered into Timneet's ear.

"Her sister? Her best friend, maybe?" Timneet responded, equally as careful to remain quiet.

Timneet jerked her head away from Miriam to hide the tears. *If I ever lost Miriam like that, I would die. There would be no screams. I would simply die.*

Miriam tugged at Timneet's wrist, grabbing a lantern with the other hand. Timneet followed Miriam to the end of the cave as she wondered, *Did we do what was right? Were we destined to fight this fight?*

***

That night, Timneet slept by Miriam's side cradling their weapons in pitch darkness.

"Miri…are you sleeping?"

"No."

"I can't help but think of Adey and Amaniel, Miri. And, Ne'Amin, his sweet face and promises of a *tomorrow*. I betrayed him, Miri. Maybe we could have stayed? I get flashes of their faces every time I close my eyes."

"Do you know what I think about before going to sleep? Do you know the only pictures that play in my mind and keep me awake? Do you know what I *feel*, Timneet?"

"What is it?"

"I don't *feel* anymore…I haven't since I saw fire eat my mother alive and there was nothing I could do to save her. But now? We can save her."

Timneet knew that *her* was their new mother, and her name was Eritrea.

***

Timneet watched as Miriam raised her arms on their newest meeting grounds, outside of a similar cave to the first one they had ever called home, flaunting her rifle in one hand and a grenade in the other. Miriam smiled madly, flashing every tooth. Two freedom fighters, their brothers in combat, Tesfa and Emba, stood perfectly still on either side of the girls, positioned to spray bullets at the slightest movement. They were guarding four captives clothed in their camouflage uniforms with a square shaped cloth of red, yellow, and green patched on their shoulders. Timneet and Miriam cradled their weapons. The black cumbersome combat boots of the regime, starkly different and heavier than the freedom fighters' plastic airy sandals, exposed them as Ethiopians while Timneet and her line remained on the ground. The capture was easy, but the mentally-ravaging part came in the kill—an act Timneet had yet to embrace in her five years of combat.

The captives sat with their bound hands behind their heads and their ankles also wrapped tightly together with cords.

"I repeat, do each of you understand, if you speak before you are permitted to do so, these bullets here," Miriam pointed to the guns Timneet and the two who had become their brothers in combat held, "will go right through your skulls? Is this clear? Your friend over there is a lovely example." She lifted her chin in the direction of the fifth soldier, slumped onto the lap of the impassive Ethiopian soldier beside him.

While the men looked to their friend, Timneet whispered in Miriam's ear, "If you're going to kill them, do it fast. Enough with the torture, Miri."

Timneet had not killed a soul. She left the job to Miriam who enjoyed instilling fear in the enemy, then ripping their mental strength to shreds before taking their lives.

"Full names. Now," Miriam demanded. She kicked the heel of the first captive's combat boot.

"Indirew Abechaw," he responded.

"Speak with sureness. You are men, are you not?" Miriam shouted.

Uncomfortable in her skin, Timneet paced in front of the seated captives, patting her thigh with her free hand, while Miriam continued to taunt their captives.

"I want to hear the same confidence you all bear in the streets of our villages when you ransack our homes," Miriam pointed forward in the air, "when you terrorize young children, burn and maim our parents, and murder hundreds of thousands of innocent people without remorse in your hearts."

None of the prisoners responded, heeding her earlier advice.

"Now, tell me, what is your *name*?" Miriam repeated, disgusted.

Timneet recognized the game Miriam was playing. It was as though Miriam was obsessed with the game the regime had played with them long ago.

"Indirew Abechaw," the soldier spoke a little louder, however, self-esteem still escaped his voice.

The others followed with their first and last names.

"Weldinsae Gersun."

"Abraham Betinaw."

The last captive remained silent. Timneet studied Miriam. She had become like the soldiers on the streets of Zigib, brewing torture for their prisoners before killing them off. Timneet's mind ran wild with thoughts. *What if on the other side of this field, Amaniel sat bound in front of Ethiopian captors, praying for his life to be spared? What if it were Ne'Amin who sat slumped across Amaniel's lap? I don't know how much more of this I can take.*

The final captive stared ahead, refusing to entertain Miriam. Timneet prayed for his barefaced disobedience. She knew what Miriam did with captives who dared to push her—taking their eyes out with the blade of a knife, shooting them once per hour from their legs up toward their chest as they screamed in agony, and the one she performed most often, setting them afire and cackling as they burned. Timneet walked away for most of the acts, only hearing about them from their brothers in combat, who retold the stories in awe of what they could never bring themselves to do.

Miriam would not allow a captive to ruin her combat team's triumph, especially now. There was mental destruction to be had, and Miriam preferred to commence immediately, ignoring the looks Timneet gave her, urging her to stop the torturous acts.

"Eritrea, the independence of this nation *is* coming, my friends. Have you noticed the increase in deaths among your men? You are losing a lot more of your soldiers, are you not? The more frequent battle losses?" Miriam dreamed aloud. She occasionally jabbed her rifle in their faces. The face of the enemy before death she often said was exhilarating to her. It was what she seemed to live for. "Oh, the victory for Eritrea will be sweet, my friends. We will make history, and then go on to have many great accomplishments. The world will admire our struggle and respect our beloved nation. Unfortunately, you four will never see it."

Timneet's brother in combat, Tesfa, hollered, "Yes!" from the background. Timneet turned around at the unexpected interjection. Tesfa stood positioned for shooting. Emba, their other brother, fixed his weapon on the face of the prisoner nearest to him, waiting for Miriam's command as instructed.

Miriam calmed Emba, "Now, now. Let's ask what they would prefer before jumping to killing. They may or may not want to live to see that day."

Timneet remembered the last time she had expressed concern over human life. Miriam had yelled, "This is war!" She followed with a reminder of Abo Solomon's words of wisdom—how they should never use their hearts. Timneet opened her mouth to join in the taunting to avoid Miriam's ridicule later.

"Do you care to see a free Eritrea? Do you? Indirew?" Timneet asked.

"Yes," Indirew responded.

"Yes, what?" Timneet demanded.

"Yes, our honorable leader."

"Our honorable leader, what?" she followed the protocol of instilling fear, but her mind flashed pictures of Amaniel and Ne'amin. She thought of Ne'Amin often since the day Berhane, their combat leader, mentioned Barka would be collaborating in the liberation effort.

"Yes, our honorable leader. I speak in the name of a liberated Eritrea." Most of Timneet's life, the regime forced her people to sing their national anthem. The day was coming when Eritrea would have an anthem of its own. It was only a matter of time and a continued streak of successful battles before the mantra, *in the name of a liberated Eritrea,* would make that dream a reality. She planted the seed in the captives' heads, forced by Miriam's eyes.

"Very good, Indirew. I see you listen," Timneet responded for Miriam to hear, turning to the last captive with his murdered friend still nestled in his lap, her heart saddening over a lost friend.

"I take it you all agree?" Miriam focused on the remaining two cooperative captives. "Friends, you will not be dying today. Unless of course, you choose not to participate in one of our favorite games. You see, we haven't even reached the exciting part yet." She tossed the grenade up in the air, catching it with her hand. "You there," she pointed to the soldier adjacent to Indirew, "Weldinsae, are you married?"

"Yes, yes, I am, our honorable leader, in the name of a free Eritrea," Weldinsae responded.

"Very good," Miriam said. This captive followed instruction, as well. "And, what is your wife's name?" Miriam asked.

"Memeresh is her name, our honorable leader, in the name of a free Eritrea." Weldinsae became visibly uncomfortable, his knees trembling, knocking against one another.

Timneet shook her head. *Please make her stop.* Her stomach began churning as she smelled murder on their hands, triggering the stench of rotting flesh.

Tesfa and Emba stepped closer.

Miriam continued, turning to Indirew. "And yours?" she asked.

"What is the point in this? What are you going to do with us?" Indirew asked.

"Oh, you have to be a little more patient than that. You cowards." Miriam looked each captive in their eyes. "You look into our eyes, into the eyes of an innocent people, and you see the horror in them, placed there by your acts of terror. But do you ever halt and spare us? Do you say to yourself, *They've pained enough*? Do you tell yourself, *Let's stop now, these are innocent children who simply want to go to school*? Does the thought, *She's been raped by four of my men, I cannot be a fifth and have any part in this,* enter your minds? Or even better, *I can't cut his hands in front of his children, they will all be scarred for life*? Has, *We can't burn these loving mothers alive and make their children watch,* ever crossed your minds?" Miriam roared her questions.

Timneet shook her head vigorously at Miriam's chilling words. The images were forever etched in her mind—a pile of her friends' bodies filled with holes, her mother, lying in a pool of blood in the courtyard of her home, her father, losing life from his hands, and the look on Miriam's face the day she come home from the marketplace where she had seen her mother perish before her eyes. Miriam's words of encouragement never left her. "There was nothing we could do then. Times are different now. The power is in our hands, Timneet," Miriam had whispered on their journey with Abo Solomon. Still, Timneet wondered if by sparing these lives they would be sparing her own brother and the only love she had ever known.

"Now, let's get back to our game," Miriam snarled. "I want you to yell, louder than the bullets firing from across the land, the names of your children and how long it has been since you last saw them." Pain washed over the captives' faces in the form of tears.

"Lechiye and Mertew, it has been two years, our honorable leader, in the name of a liberated Eritrea," Indirew responded.

"Densen, three years since I've seen my son, our honorable leader, in the name of a liberated Eritrea," Weldinsae followed.

"I have no children, our honorable leader, in the name of a liberated Eritrea," claimed the third captive.

The last of the captives remained quiet and still.

The voices of those who spoke quivered. Miriam smirked, while Timneet frowned and was moved to tears, picturing her mother lying in the courtyard. After Miriam's first few killings, Timneet had realized that revenge wouldn't cleanse the great sadness that stifled her soul. Only life and preservation of it would set them free. She argued often that they should imprison their captives and hold them in bondage for years instead of committing murder. But Timneet's ideas were always met with disdain, receiving answers from her combat team that raised good points. "Do you think they would do the same for us? Or, do you think their orders are to kill on sight?" her brothers and sisters in combat would ask.

"One last question, and because the majority of you have cooperated, I promise to let you all depart after I receive the answers to my very last request. Here is the challenge—in order for that to happen, I must receive an answer from all four of you. Let's start with you, the silent one." Miriam walked to the quiet one, Timneet following her. The grin on Miriam's face expanded. Tesfa and Emba beside Timneet caught the contagious smile. "How old are you?" Miriam asked, Timneet crouching by her side. They locked eyes with the prisoner. With less than a hand's length between their noses, the prisoner spit in Timneet's face.

Before Timneet could even react to a brazen move, another captive tried to redeem the group by giving Miriam the answer she sought, "He is eighteen!"

Timneet took the number in. Unexpectedly, it was her own age. She rose and backed away from the group, wiping the saliva with her sleeve. Tesfa and Emba rushed and tackled the prisoner, beating him with their fists. The captive, bound by rope on his hands and feet, lay on his back and took the strikes, yielding very few cries to make it stop.

"Stop! Lift him up," Timneet screamed at the rough nature of her combat brothers' force.

Miriam faced the captive and slapped him with the back of her hand. "Eighteen? Is that right?"

The captive panted in his seat while supported upright by Tesfa and Emba. Despite the thrashing, he offered no words.

Miriam stood straight and turned toward the cave where the rest of their combat team was preparing for mealtime.

"Now, Miriam?" Tesfa called.

As she walked farther away, Miriam gave a signal to her soldiers —flicking her wrist twice above her head with one upright finger.

"No!" Timneet yelled, but her brothers seemed to not have heard, or they were ignoring her as Miriam often advised them to do.

Tesfa and Emba stepped back. Eighteen bullets ambushed the prisoner's body. All hope vanished from the faces of the remaining three soldiers of the regime.

"In the name of a liberated Eritrea," Miriam rejoiced.

Within a single moment, the whistle of a grenade sounded in the air. Timneet looked to Miriam, who had turned toward them suddenly, wide-eyed and confused.

"Miri, is that your—," Timneet began to ask, until the ground flew from beneath her feet. An explosion sent the four freedom fighters flying to the ground several meters away from where they stood with the captives. Timneet fell to her face, sending a stinging pain to her cheek and the palms on which she landed. She opened her eyes, seeing crumbles of ground before her and the body of her closest friend lying still.

Invasion! Timneet thought, panicking. *Grab Miri and run!* she yelled at her body to cooperate, only she was paralyzed with fear.

"Miri," Timneet mumbled, moving her legs with uncertainty. "Miri," she repeated to the back of Miriam's head. The sounds of Amharic rushed to their sides, the language of Ethiopians, confirming Timneet's first thought.

Where did they come from? How did they find our grounds? Will the others hear in time to save us? Save us!

A soldier with red, yellow, and green patched to his arm turned Miriam toward Timneet.

"Are they alive?" another bellowed from the distance.

Miriam's head fell to the ground, as the soldier forced her chin to face Timneet. She opened her eyes more to find Miriam's ajar and her chest unmoving, the stillness on her face sending a stabbing pain to Timneet's heart, sending unstoppable tremors throughout her entire body.

"No, this one isn't!" the soldier responded.

The tears rolled down Timneet's face and met the ground beneath her cheek as the soldier with colors on his arm dragged Miriam by her collar, her chin dangling onto her chest.

"Bring her anyway…and the others, too!"

***

Timneet regained consciousness, brought back to life by the sounds of unfamiliar voices.

Where am I? How long have I been here?

"What do you think those big cigarettes from Cuba taste like, Fetlew?" a monotonous voice inquired. "I hear they are amazing, comrade."

"How would you know, Haileabu?" the other questioned in the midst of catching his breath from laughing.

"I *said*, I hear, not I know." Haileabu retorted.

Fetlew? Haileabu? Who? I am in the presence of the regime? Where are those voices coming from? Where am I? Timneet opened her eyes—her legs lay before her, forcefully straight atop a dirt floor. She pressed her lower back flat against a sturdily built wall and strained to lift her head. *Look up*, she urged. She could not even move. Alarmed, Timneet focused on her feet. Her ankles throbbed from the swelling. The cords used to tighten them together were barely visible, hidden by the overlapping inflammation of her skin. Timneet examined her hands more closely. She was missing nails on two of her fingers on her right hand. The nail beds of the remaining fingers were punctured on her left.

Who is responsible for this? How long have I been here? How is it that I am no longer on the field? What in the world has happened? Timneet battled her memory for answers, and frantically, she tried to retrace her steps.

The deafening bark of the men began to escalate as they laughed hysterically at each other's jokes.

Timneet raised her shoulders and lifted her chest, raising her gaze in the process. The smell of cigarettes, rotting flesh, and feces penetrated her nose. Narrow, tall metal bars stood between herself and the outside world, barricading her from all of freedom. She assessed the room and confronted the ugly truth—the demise of her combat team. To her left and right lay the bodies and familiar faces, some stooped over others, of her cherished brothers and sisters in battle. Rezene, Goitom, Tesfa, and Emba were among forty others who surrounded Timneet, lifeless.

This cannot be! My sight is deceiving me. She silently spoke to her eyes, *Why would you trick me in such a way?*

Timneet struggled against the tightly knotted cords that captivated her limbs. *There must be an escape,* she thought. She searched the walls and dirt floor for holes, but there was no exit route in sight.

"This is how it ends?" The sound of her own voice made Timneet lonely. *This is how it feels to know you are going to die?*

And the thought that had failed to reach her before hit her suddenly, harder than the throbbing pain that consumed her. *Where is Miriam? The blast—we were attacked. Miriam's eyes…her body was not moving. He said we were dead. Why would he say that? The* thoughts grew less fragmented as realization settled in.

She scanned each body for more clues, and as her eyes traveled the room, a flash of blue caught her attention. The awkwardly hanging neck snapped to the side nearly sent her soul to heaven. The little sun that crept through the bars of the tiny window above shone on the pendant around Miriam's neck as it dangled on the shoulder of another. Dry blood formed a layer on the side of Miriam's face, her mouth gaping open. Laying two bodies away, Miriam was gone. Timneet would never hear her voice again, her embrace would never again console Timneet's fears.

Timneet fought the lump in her throat as Miriam would have ordered her to do. She pushed her seat closer to her dear friend, ignoring the stabbing pain through her rear end on the rough floor. When she arrived by Miriam's side, Timneet kissed her dearest friend's forearm, leaving her lips on her cold flesh. *Miriay, Miriay, how could you leave me like this?* Unintentionally, she let out a whimper, suppressing the weeping she would have surely released had she been in the presence of friends and not the enemy.

How long have we been here? Oh, my dear Miri. You never deserved this.

"Fetlew, tanks!" The alarm in the guard's voice suggested they were not tanks of the Ethiopian regime. The roaring sound came closer.

The two soldiers in a room adjacent the prison cell shuffled their feet in a hurry, heading past the cell and toward what Timneet deemed an exit. Timneet lay low, attempting to stay inconspicuous among her brothers and sisters. She played dead, closing her eyes. If those were Eritrean freedom fighters in the tanks outside, the regime would want to make sure they killed all Eritrean captives. Her heart pounded as she hoped there would be no time to confirm all were dead.

"Get out, Haileabu! Faster!" Their footsteps echoed as they ran through the corridor.

Timneet raised her head, straining her neck, and watched the action from the corner of her cell. The soldiers walked backwards with their hands in the air, surrendering. Freedom fighters barged in, propping their army weapons ahead of their chests with their shoulders resting behind their ears, ordering the soldiers to the ground.

"Get down now!" they yelled.

It was a sight that would have made any human being shed tears, especially one held captive.

"Is anyone alive in there?" shouted a voice.

"Over here," Timneet mumbled among the bodies.

"There! Did you hear that?" another freedom fighter asked, pointing at Timneet's corner.

A young man retrieved the key to the cell from the belt of the guard whose face squealed underneath the foot of a freedom fighter. Timneet whimpered loudly enough to be heard amongst the silenced bodies until blurs for faces approached. The soldiers freed Timneet from the several cords of bondage and her hands flew to rub at the raw imprints on her wrists. A freedom fighter swept her from the ground and carried her out the prison cell.

"You are in good hands, sister," a young man decorated with a string of bullets across his chest assured her.

The rest of the soldiers restrained the two prison guards, taking rope to their hands and feet. The freedom fighters, Timneet, and the two prison guards stepped out into the world, Timneet's combat family on the backs of the rescuing soldiers. The sun pierced her eyes, and when they adjusted to the beaming rays, Timneet was in awe of all that surrounded her. Several freedom fighters in military trucks greeted her. A young fighter left the driver's seat. He expanded the back of the truck and made room for Timneet to lie down. As the solider placed her gently on the truck, the driver stared at her, calling, "Timneet? Timneet? Timneet!"

Dear God, she thought. She physically opened her mouth but found not a single word would exit. The young fighter facing her found himself in the same predicament. Before uttering a word, Timneet, in disbelief, placed her hands on the soldier's face and patted his cheeks.

I am dead, she reasoned. It was the only explanation for the last hour of her life, from the rescue until this very moment when Ne'Amin was calling her name.

"Let's move! They will arrive any minute now. Ne'Amin, drive," a soldier ordered.

As they settled in their seats, the soldier questioned, "Ne'Amin, is this your sister?"

"No," he replied, staring at Timneet through the rearview mirror, "she's my wife."

Chapter 7

Narrated by Ma'arinet Neguse

Life can only be understood backwards;
but it must be lived forwards.
—Søren Kierkegaard

"You home for four *mons* and you still living like *zis* one?" my mother asked me, scanning the mess that had become my room and dragging her feet through the clothes on the floor to emphasize her point. Four months since my days of freedom began, since leaving Esak. Most nights in the first month of being back in my parent's home were met with screams into my pillow as I cried over my children that would never set foot in this world. The pain of remembering my babies splattered on my sheets got so bad that in grieving, I pulled patches of hair from my scalp as I stifled my cries in bed at night.

I soon managed to shed the pain with the help of thoughts like, *They're better off not knowing their father.* And, in those thoughts, I found peace—that my children were blessed to be where they were, in heaven and as far away from their cruel and heartless father as could be. Serenity had warmed my every day after my line of thinking changed, placing me in the position to thank God for keeping my children with Him because He knew they would face more harm at the hands of their earthly father had they lived.

Esak had visited my school once after I moved out of our apartment, standing outside one of my classrooms until I warned him I would file for a restraining order. I never heard from him after that day, although Sarsum did hear from her mother that he had grown to be double his size and had checked into a rehabilitation facility for alcoholics. I shrugged when I heard the news. He was no longer any concern of mine.

"Yes, Mom, but I'll tell you what—I'm a lot happier living out of these boxes and in *this* craziness." I spared my parents the details about why it ended with Esak. They never even knew of my failed pregnancies. I cherished them too much to cause them the same pain I had felt over the years, and I knew that exposing the truth of my life with Esak, would cause them just that. Instead, I told them, "He wasn't the right one for me." Surprisingly they accepted it and asked me no questions. I was convinced that Sarsum's mother must have reached out to my parents and helped them understand that they wouldn't have had a breathing daughter had I not come home when I did.

"Ma'arinet, look at *zis* one," my mother cooed, pulling a photo album buried beneath a box of clothes. "I love *zis peectures*. You always make me smile *end* look good," she said. Since my return, my parents welcomed the idea of having a photographer for a daughter. I think it was the realization of them almost losing me that made them reconsider their harsh words the day I revealed my passion two years before. I, on the other hand, continued my schooling as though they applauded my efforts hoping that they someday would —and lo and behold, it took Esak for that to happen.

"Let me get *zat*." My mother hurried to pick up the ringing phone from her bedroom. "Ma'arinet," she sang my name a minute later, "Sarsum for you."

I met her in her room and took hold of the receiver. "Hey Sar," I said as my mother left to give me privacy.

"So, I have a big problem on my hands, Maar."

"What's wrong?" I asked, a bit alarmed.

"They...are...garbage!" Sarsum yelled.

"First of all, that is my ear." Sarsum was only going through a male-bashing phase. "Calm down."

"I can't stand it, Maari. You know I hate cheating bastards. There is nothing...in...this...world...I...hate...more!" I could imagine Sarsum pounding her fists on the dining room table at home, finishing off a tub of cookie dough ice cream throughout her tantrum.

"Sar, why are you acting a fool? *What* is the problem?"

"Eritrean men are—"

"Whoa. Don't do that. It does you no good to bash every man based on the acts of one idiot, especially throwing generalizations out there. What about your brother? Aahkli is a stand up guy. And...and if he, and your dad, and my dad, and all of our Eritrean male cousins are brilliant and loving, then you have to know that you will find a man that resembles the good in them."

"But—"

"Sarsum, you have to believe it's possible. Not only that—you have to believe you're worth an Eritrean man of that caliber. Sar, claim it!"

Damn, I sure am good. Thank God I actually believe my words.

"I hear you, Maari, and I know it's not right of me. I'm just so sick of it all—the whole *show*. They run around shouting 'Eritrea!' from the mountaintops, and what do I get? Cheated on!"

"That's not just Eritrean men. That could be any man. Hell, it could be any woman! You already know that not all Eritrean men are like that, like Adgi." Sarsum's boyfriend of three years, Adgi, cheated on her on countless occasions. "Sar, you know better than to blame them for his mistakes. Besides, I'm sure women all over the world feel the same exact way with the men of *their* ethnicities. You are not the only one who goes through this. I guess the answer is if you want a man from where you're from, find one who makes you feel like a queen. And, if where he comes from doesn't matter to you, again, find one who treats you like an empress." I rotated my wrist in the air as though summoning for more wine, envisioning myself amongst fellow royalty. "But," I warned my friend, "Sar, you have to also be willing to treat him like your king. I'm not talking about Adgi, either. Move on already, and give the next man the best of you."

"Shut up and tell me your secret. Maari, how do you remain positive after all Esak's done to you?"

"No one's perfect, Sar. Not me and definitely not Esak. Do you really want to know how I stay in good spirits?"

"*Uhh*, yeah," Sarsum weighed in, her sarcasm forcing a smile to my face.

I looked to the ceiling and my smile grew even wider. "I forgave." I was met with silence, but I continued anyway. "I forgave, and the world got a lot more comfortable to live and breathe in."

"So, you're saying I should just forgive Adgi?"

"First leave, Sar. Forgiveness can happen from a distance and when you follow through, be prepared to live a life far better than you ever dreamed possible. It'll only happen when you make moves, though. So as your sister, just as you were my voice of reason, I'm telling you to get out and move on. There is a world of *amazingness* waiting for you!" I hoped she could hear the giddiness in my voice as a testament to what she could look forward to in her future without Adgi. I knew she was tired, as I had been with Esak, of living in misery.

When we ended the call, Sarsum's question lingered in my mind, and I promised I would one day succeed in making her understand. She was deserving of far better.

As I twiddled the phone cord between my fingers, I heard my mother in panic. "Ma'arinet! Ma'arinet! Come here, now!"

I poked my head out from their room, preparing for the worst as my father chimed in, "Ma'arinet!"

I emerged from my parent's bedroom, still in the corridor, frightened at what I would find. "Are you guys okay?" The last time I heard my mother scream that way it revolved around the story of my birth.

"Ma'arinet, hurry, now!" My father's voice thundered through the halls, at which point I ran to the living room.

"What's wrong? What happened?" Their faces were pale as they sat with their mouths wide open, paralyzed with their hands stuck in the air pointing to the television, the remote control still in my father's hand. The mascara smeared on my mother's face ruined her soft features, making her look like a weeping widow.

I hesitated in watching the program that had captivated my parents, temporarily ruining their ability to speak. All it took was a frustrated, "Look at *za* tv!" from my father before I whipped my head around and watched Eritrea on international news.

Next to a British reporter's head, in the top right corner of the screen, an image of northeast Africa appeared from a square. It was not an ordinary map. *This* map had a squiggly line—a mark never seen before. It was the line for which every Eritrean longed, whether they were fighting in the struggle or they found themselves displaced from the war in a far away land—it was the line of demarcation, separating Eritrea from Ethiopia.

"Oh dear God," my mother finally spoke, exhaling through her mouth with each word.

The square image expanded into footage of Eritrean freedom fighters parading with their weapons in the air as they danced in the streets of Asmara. Army tanks flooded the city in droves, and women, both young and old, flocked to the soldiers, kissing them and hanging on their necks.

"I never *sought* I see *zis* one," my father said in one breath. "*Eretraya*, the newest African nation, has gained its independence after a gruesome thirty year war with neighboring Ethiopia. Conflict began in the region in 1961…" I lost concentration in the words and focused on the sight of a free Eritrea. People were crying and shrieking in the middle of the streets. Drivers honked their horns and women and children bombarded the incoming marching soldiers with popcorn and songs of jubilation.

My father sobbed. I sank to the floor and joined in the celebratory tears of an ended struggle and restoration of calm. I knew I would remember the day for many years and most especially the words conveyed by my parents when the commotion settled in our home.

"Ma'arinet," my mother began, "Neguse *end* me feel you need to go to Eritrea soon."

"By myself?" I asked, barely remembering anything from my childhood.

"Yes, Ma'arinet," my father continued for my mother as it seemed too difficult for her to finish a conversation they had obviously rehearsed. "It is time you discover *za trus* about your family *end za* years before we took you."

"But *you're* my family," I demanded, not wanting to face the truth my father spoke of, and forgetting for a moment that it was *my* dream to return when Eritrea was free and unearth my roots.

My mother disappeared and shortly returned with a letter in her hand. "You will take *zis* one *wiz* you. When we buy your ticket, my sister, Kibra, is wait in Eritrea for you. We talk about *zis* day for many years."

And, just like that, I was persuaded to go and live out my dream of uncovering the details of my early years and document it all. It was a monumental time in my life, and my greatest joy was knowing that my camera would help capture it all.

**

August 17, 1991

Dear Me,

I am on a plane. Yes, on a plane. This is amazing. Which part? All of it. Pick any part of my life, and you've got your answer right there. I've learned quite a lot in the last few months, but most importantly I've learned a thing or two about this world we live in. When I lost each child, my precious babies, my soul suffered a pain I wouldn't wish on my worst enemy. But do you know how I was restored, how my eyes changed after Esak took them from me? I cherished life, with every fiber of my being, like never before. I can sit here and tell you all of the things that have gone so drastically wrong and caused me countless sleepless nights, but what good would that do for my eighty-year-old self who'll read this and be moved to tears by how depressed I sound. Why would I give my eighty-year-old self any reason to cry over how I've handled the woes and tribulations that have managed to creep into my world, causing me to regret how I chose to live and speak about this life? I want the elderly me to look back on the young me and jump out of my rocking chair and dance when I look through all these pictures I've taken. I want to be in awe over how I made magic with the chaos and turned it all into a gorgeous bouquet of roses. My past and the scars that come from it do not own me, and I have been free to live wonderfully since I came to that realization. I want the future me to nod feverishly at every page from here on out decorated with photographs of life and beauty until the arthritis in my neck forces me to stop. I want you to be proud of me. So, here's me…in all of my glory.

I haven't set pen to paper in a long time, probably since high school when my first camera became my new pen, but I wanted to write you today to share some pretty hefty news—I am FREE. I'm writing from the skies. This plane is going I don't know how many miles per hour, and time and time again throughout this ride, I've imagined myself grabbing the airplane microphone from the stewardess and telling the whole plane that I am ALIVE and WELL. I think it's important that all of these strangers know this—although not as important as making sure I'm not hauled off by airport security when we land, but I digress. I just stopped writing for a minute to read each capitalized word, and just in case you're wondering, I feel as strongly reading them as I did writing them. Truth feels so divinely good. I want to dance through the aisles, and I want to wake the old couple sleeping right by me so they can join me in a Greek huddle of footwork. Something on the inside won't let me stop laughing, and the smiling —forget about it. My cheeks hurt from all the smiling. I'm free in a world that has all sorts of answers, everywhere I turn, and all I have to do is stay positive and keep my faith alive that these answers will find their way to me. In the midst of my search for answers to my birth story, I must keep my faith, and I will not let anything come in between us—not fear, doubt, or negativity. There's simply no time or energy for any of that. Not in my world, at least.

My adoption was a heavy load my parents carried for most of my life, and the weight reflected in their eyes the day they shared the news. I remember writing about it at sixteen—the whole family dynamics —until my fingers calloused and I had no more words to share. I still can't believe all of this is happening to me. I know that whatever comes of this trip, it is all meant to help complete the full circle of my life, so I must be careful to reject anger if it ever tries to interfere— anger doesn't exactly fit in the circle, anyway. One thing is for sure— letting my relationship with Esak go is one of the best gifts I've ever given myself. It's one that I know I deserved in its entirety. Although he had put me in a world of mourning for lost life, the lives of my precious children, I still recognize that blessings have rained on me since I chose to leave, making all kinds of noise in the downpour. For that, I am forever grateful.

Thank goodness for open tickets, the smartest decision I could've made. I don't know how long I'll be gone, but the time away will be days spent wisely. It'll allow me the time I need to get this research underway and really understand where I come from. I'll finally be able to rest knowing that I'll have, hopefully, completed the story of my beginnings, the story of my life.

I placed the pen in the folds of my journal and moved to return the heavy book of pictures and entries to my carry-on below the seat at my feet. The elderly couple beside me had fallen asleep around the same time my admiration for them had begun. The older man, in his seventies I guessed, had laid his head on his wife's shoulder who sat in her window seat, and her cheek rested on his bald creased head, a position they probably had grown to love. I thought about my eighty-year-old self and how soul-nourishing it would someday be to have an undying love and such security knowing that love would be this good. I thought it would make for a beautiful photograph, and I could not resist having it for memory's sake.

I eased my camera out from its bag and from my window seat I snapped a few photos of the unsuspecting couple sitting in the two seats next to me. I found myself not caring about their privacy as it was *their* obligation, I believed, to share their secret on lasting love through an involuntary photo. *How amazing it is to be reminded of love*, I thought. *How incredibly beautiful. I have to show Reid and Drea these pictures when I get back. I have to let them see what they'll look like years from now.*

I raised my glass to the couple who was clueless as to the inspiration they provided another human being while they lay fast asleep. I wondered how many people I compelled to smiles while I slept, and the thought alone made me chuckle.

A simulation of the plane on the monitor straight ahead attached to the back of my front neighbor's seat reappeared. An X marked the city of Chicago followed by a line attached to the plane which was now, as I eagerly watched, flying over western Europe. I caught myself taking long deep inhalations as the thrill of bringing my past alive was, at times, too great for my lungs to stand.

I was on a flight to a home I had long forgotten, and yet, it was a home which proffered me a peace like I had never experienced. The mere thought of learning about my roots and possibly reuniting with my birth parents' families, a feat Aunt Kibra promised we would try to achieve, was an invaluable treasure that no one could ever steal.

The plane began its descent. Home was but a few more stops away.

***

When we landed in Eritrea the following morning, I hurried off the plane but not as rapidly as the woman behind me who nearly pushed me onto the tarmac. The woman dressed in the traditional *zuria*, with her *netsella* wrapped around her head, landed on her feet and then on her knees as she belted out a cry of celebration and praise, "*elelelelelelelel*," a cry I had only heard at weddings back in Chicago. She raised her hands to the sky and kissed the ground a number of times like a Muslim in devotional prayer. With my camera dangling from my neck, I removed the cap and snapped away at such a beautiful sight of a woman who had probably been away from home for many years. *Click*.

It was a matter of minutes before the airport security, two Eritrean men, raised her from the ground and patted her back with smiles. "Welcome home, dear mother," they shared, holding her by her elbows and guiding her inside. I captured the backs of the three, the elderly woman and the soldiers on either side.

I reached the inside of the airport and was greeted by a multitude of flies. I swatted them and marveled at the officials who walked about as though the bothersome insects did not exist.

"Next!" an official yelled.

I reached the desk and supplied my passport and visa.

"How long are you staying?"

"I have an open ticket, sir," I replied in broken Tigrinya to which he chuckled.

"Welcome home," he said with a nod and a smile, "and, I hope your Tigrinya gets better during your stay."

I grinned, feeling my cheeks burning. He stamped my passport and directed me to the baggage area where he pointed to two public phones. "Use those if you need to call your family."

Aunt Kibra and I had already agreed before my departure that I would take a taxi cab to her home. She did not have a vehicle, and there was no way I would ask her to take the bus an hour away to reach me.

I grabbed my two human-sized pieces of luggage and with the help of an airport guard placed them on a cart. The same guard then went out of his way to assist me to the taxi stand flooded with cabs and a massive bus that was quickly overflowing with passengers from my plane and what seemed like factory workers from nearby.

As I climbed into the back seat of the taxi, the driver asked, "What are you doing? Come here to the front, my child," he urged. "It is custom to sit with the driver. The back seat is only used when the front is full."

"Oh, I'm so sorry. I didn't know." I entered the passenger's side and sat with my camera on my lap.

"Where to, my child?" the man asked.

"Genesaba." I declared the name of Aunt Kibra's village.

"That's an hour away." He sounded surprised.

"I know."

"That will be 300 nakfa."

I looked for the cab's meter or a sign that would give rates. I soon realized pricing was to their discretion, and I really had no choice but to agree, not having anything to compare it to.

"My aunt will pay you when we arrive."

"Very well," he said. "Off to Genesaba, then."

We began the hour long ride to see my Aunt Kibra for the very first time. My heart fluttered the more dirt road we covered. I kept having to wipe my palms on my jeans. *What is she going to think of me? Am I what she's expecting? What if my Tigrinya isn't as good as I hoped and communicating with her is impossible?*

When my foot tapping on the car mat caught the stares of the cab driver, I stopped, taking a deep breath in and exhaling as Drea had taught me to do in times of stress. I brought the strap of my camera over my head as I usually wore it, like a necklace, and held it in my hands as I looked through the lens to keep my nerves calm—it was my best friend on the drive. Behind my lens lay a world that reminded me I wasn't in America anymore, distracting me from what was to come.

My first few pictures were of a boy without a leg or arm on the same side of his body, confined to a wheelchair which was pushed by a girl who looked his age. They laughed as they raced down the street. *Landmine?* I wondered. Back in Chicago we had discussed the buried explosives, or "devils in the ground," as my parents often called them. They had said landmines were a constant fear on our way to Sudan, as they knew many friends who lost their limbs and some even their lives as a result of one wrong step.

Click.

Abruptly the driver stopped as emaciated cattle stormed the street followed by a man with a whip flailing his arms around, yelling, "Move out of the way!" Passersby ran as fast as they could away from the spectacle as the man tried to gain control of his livestock with more thrashes. There obviously were no organizations like Animal Cruelty on this side of the world.

Click.

While stopped, a number of children swarmed my side of the cab holding boxes to my window, shrieking, "Gum, tissue for sale." I wondered what Sarsum would think of this. We were both deprived from Girl Scouts because our parents thought we would be kidnapped in the midst of selling cookies door to door, and yet children younger than we had been were on the streets hawking candy and napkins. There was clearly no worry of kidnapping in Eritrea. *I bet our parents would have loved raising us here,* I thought as I chuckled at their adorable faces.

I shook my head to the children and said, "No, thank you," as we began moving again when the cattle had cleared the road. I caught the children's shining faces in still form with my camera poised in my palm and looking through the back windshield as they ran behind us laughing.

Click.

Fifteen minutes or so had passed before another hardened brake pushed me against the seat belt across my chest as the driver pounded on the pedal and parked the car behind another in the middle of the street. "Get out," he urged. He faced the government building across the road adorned with the new Eritrean flag waving high on a pole. He placed his hand on his chest and I hurried to the driver side alongside him, mimicking his moves. He stared at the flag in silence. The tune of the national anthem blared through invisible speakers while all the men, women, and children on the street stood still as far as I could see. With my right hand firmly on my heart, I used my left to snap pictures of the road of allegiance. I figured if I was caught for disrespecting the moment, I could blame it on being a foreigner.

Click. Click. Click.

We arrived at Aunt Kibra's home shortly after, and my stomach began to flip as I stood outside her door wondering what it was I should say. The driver, who waited in the cab behind me, grew impatient and honked his horn, causing Aunt Kibra to fling her door open.

"Ma'arinet!" she screamed. "Oh, I've waited for this day for years!" Her hug was so firm, she tricked my lungs into coughing.

"Aunt Kibra, it's so nice to finally meet you!" I exclaimed, young children hugging my legs as I held onto my aunt. "Are you Natsa and Michael?" I asked. They were names I had known for years as my cousins, but never had any images for their faces.

"Yes, these are your cousins, my child." Aunt Kibra took a look at the cab and asked me, "How much is it?"

"It's 300 nakfa, but I only have American which I'll give you of course."

"300 nakfa!" she screamed. In a dash, she was at the driver's window. "You should be ashamed of yourself taking advantage of a young girl!" She threw money into the car through his window and yelled, "Now get away from here before I summon my dead husband to haunt you!" Aunt Kibra's husband had been a general, killed during the war, his body never recovered. I did not know what she meant by her warning to the driver, nor did I want to after I saw the way he accelerated his car almost flying off the rocky road to get away.

"How much did you give him?" I asked when Aunt Kibra returned.

"I gave him 20 nakfa *after* giving ourselves a discount of 30 for him lying to you like that," she guffawed.

I followed her inside her home, a one-room abode with a tin roof, fit for herself and her two children. The Eritrean flag, a gorgeous fabric of red, blue, green, and yellow for its wreath at the center, was the curtain that separated their bedroom from the rest of the house. They had a family dog locked in a metal box in the corner of the kitchen who growled at the sound of my voice, until Aunt Kibra took a broom to his home, banging the door to settle the dog and bring peace.

"Sit, sit," Aunt Kibra urged as my cousins, no older than nine and ten, took my hands and guided me to the bench in the living area. "You're so big," she exclaimed, expanding her arms to the side. "Stay exactly how you are. Skinny is bad, Ma'arinet. You don't want to be like me."

I thought of Sarsum again. She and I had struggled with our weight since we were little, probably one of the largest reasons for us growing so close to one another. *Sarsum would love to live in a land where we were praised for our weight, rather than destroyed for it. I wish she were here to listen and see all of this!*

***

One month into the search for relatives of my birth parents and anyone who may have known my birth story, and Aunt Kibra was still a firecracker. Her motivation led me to wake up each morning with one thought while still in bed, *My work continues today.* I took a moment and looked at the ceiling as I had done every morning since my arrival. I was in a wonderful place. I was the catalyst for my own transformation, and the realization of such an important role was remarkable. I was on my way.

This is it. Everything will work in my favor, because I am supposed to be here, and the answers will come to me when they are meant to be heard. It was my daily mantra. Gratitude poured into my heart each time I spoke the words of power and purpose.

"At least we have a lead now." Aunt Kibra was relentless, accompanying me on every trip and translating when the locals' Tigrinya became too intricate for my ear drums.

I sat between her feet while she oiled my hair, massaged my scalp, and uplifted my spirits. "Not to worry my child," she reassured me, "today, you *will* find answers." Her confidence never wavered, even in the midst of dead ends.

The planes soared in the skies while I ducked for cover, hiding my ears between my knees. I had not yet acclimated to thunder without rain.

"They still get me, too. Sometimes I think a missile will fall from above. These are for celebration," my aunt whispered. "Very different." She waved her hands in the air as if she were shooing the memories of past attacks.

In thirty days time, Aunt Kibra and I visited three area hospitals in Unah, near the grounds of the once standing shelter I lived in for the first few years of my life. We interrogated a number of directors and supervisors, picking the brains of many, trying to find the one with the sharpest memory. I appreciated the interest from the administration at each hospital after I revealed the letter written by the woman who gave me life. But it was not until the second month of my journey and the fourth hospital we visited that we finally found promising words from a woman who advised us to seek the counsel of the staff at a nearby hospital called "Jigna."

***

"How can I help you? Are you hurt?" The young woman checked my aunt and me for wounds, lifting our arms and touching the backs of our legs until I objected to what would have been assault back in Chicago.

"Please don't touch me, there is nothing wrong with us." The young woman, either an inexperienced hospital aide or mental case waiting to happen, looked at me as though she had never seen a face like mine.

"We're here to see your hospital director. Is he available?" My Tigrinya was good, but I was reminded of how awful my Americanized version was by the raised eyebrows every time I started to speak. I wanted to blurt out what brought me there and the frustration with the process of eliminating one hospital after another, but I was ashamed of speaking aloud because of my accent. Although, had someone in the corridor overhead my story and knew information that could have helped me, it would have turned my life around at that very moment. Then again, no one was paying attention to me. The lobby teemed with ill patients gripping their bodily injuries and screaming in sheer pain.

"The only one here today," the aide responded looking everywhere but directly at me, "is the nursing director, and *she* is in a meeting." She searched the doorway for injured transports and seemed uninterested in our healthy bodies.

"We'll just come back tom—," I started to say, disheartened by another setback.

"We'll wait," Aunt Kibra snarled, nearly leaping at the woman who looked younger than I.

After an hour of my aunt staring at the young woman behind the counter and my feet aching from the standing, a door flung open next to us, revealing who I presumed to be the nursing director. She was dressed in white from head to toe, including a white diamond shaped uniform hat with a strip of red ribbon around its brim. The young woman who searched us before was missing her ribbon and if it had anything to do with professionalism or honorable service, I could certainly see why.

"Zahara, send any patients that have not been seen directly to my office. Tekle, Haddish, Cha'ai and Gere are up to their ears with paperwork." The director walked busily to the desk stacked with colorful binders and retrieved a number of files.

The unhelpful nursing aide pointed to us with her head and cleared her throat. "*They* want to see you," she said.

I waited for the whispers and gawking of the director and her assistant to subside—it seemed like fascination, but I didn't have time to entertain their wonder. I knew they knew I was an American. I had gotten the looks before as people scanned my clothing, even though I was casual as everyone else in jeans and a t-shirt.

I finally heard an ounce of decency come from Zahara in a, surprisingly, helpful tone. "Right this way." Zahara led my aunt and me to the director's office while the director stayed behind. It almost felt as though she were watching us as we walked away.

"Director Almaz will be right with you," Zahara whispered in the hallway at the top of the staircase. She left us in front of the director's closed door. They were probably gossiping more downstairs in the entrance where we first met Zahara. The hallway was much quieter than downstairs. I could breathe easier in a corridor of closed office doors with no one staring me down.

Shortly after, Director Almaz made her way up the same staircase, greeting us with smiles. Before the director even had the chance to open the door to her office, the words rushed from my mouth. "Look, I don't know if you can help me, but I am desperately hoping you can."

Director Almaz invited us inside with her hands. "We only have twenty minutes. Your timing is perfect. I'm on a lunch break." She patted my back and motioned us to have a seat in chairs piled with patient files and records. "Have a seat," she insisted.

Finally, a seat! But, where? I looked to Aunt Kibra whose darting eyes shared the same concern.

"Put those on the ground," the director announced, saving us from asking. She remained standing.

How noble, I thought.

"I lost my parents when I was young," I began. "I lived in an or-phanage which was also a shelter not far from here, operated by a woman named Milen. My parents—I have two loving parents, Neguse and Nigisti, and this," I turned to my aunt, "is my adoptive mother's beautiful sister, Kibra." I was rambling, successfully delaying what I feared I would hear as I had at the other hospitals, "I'm sorry, we wish we could help you."

"Child, how can I assist you?" Director Almaz interrupted.

I don't think you even can. I quickly changed my thoughts. *Stop it, Maari. Stay positive. She can help. Or, she'll find someone who can.* I was a hopeful woman on a mission. I would not allow any doubtful thoughts to deter me.

"Director Almaz, I am simply looking for answers as to where I may have been born, and it is my intention to discover relatives I may have."

My aunt brought a tissue to her face, and I knew better than to look her way. If my waterworks began, they would not stop.

"You see, my mother wrote a letter." I handed Director Almaz the only piece linking me to my birth mother. I watched the director's face for any reaction as she took the letter, unfolding it immediately. I had watched many faces before the director's, and I knew the look that resulted in disappointment. It was promising Director Almaz did not wear that same face in the first few minutes of reading. She strained for most of the letter as the writing had faded over the years and only a few words per line were legible.

"I know it is difficult to make out a number of the words." The inflection in my voice changed wildly as I described the previous hospitals I visited within the region. "You're the first to even take the time to make out the words," I continued, leaning forward on my chair with my rear barely on the edge of the seat, my heart leaping with anticipation.

Director Almaz gave no response and seemed to not even be listening, in a world of her own, seemingly trying to recollect her thoughts.

"Can you tell me of anyone who may be able to help me?" I asked, not really expecting a response. I watched for a reaction, anything to give me an idea of where I stood.

Director Almaz slowly sat in her chair almost missing her seat completely as though spirits had entered the room. She stared in the direction of the office window.

When I finished speaking and Director Almaz did not start, I waited patiently in my seat. The silence was uncomfortable, and I turned to my aunt for help.

"Director Almaz, did you understand her?" my aunt asked, leaning closer toward the director's desk.

The director nodded, still fixed on a space near the window.

I paused. I let go of fear. I surrendered. And, I waited. *I've put in hard work. Lord knows I have. But now, these answers will find me—not the other way around*, I thought.

The director set her eyes on me as if I weren't real. Her eyebrows moved up and down in what seemed like confusion and doubt. At long last, Director Almaz came to speak after several moments of silence.

"Child, what did you say your name was?" she asked.

"I didn't. It's Ma'arinet, ma'am," I searched for a reaction, "my name is Ma'arinet Neguse."

Director Almaz allowed another long pause to pass before she closed her gaping mouth and stared with no words to explain her behavior. She cupped both hands over her eyes in utter disbelief and sobbed like a motherless newborn.

CHAPTER 8

The price of anything is the amount of life you exchange for it.
—Henry David Thoreau

"When you left, a large part of me died." All through the night of her rescue from prison, Ne'Amin continued to feed Timneet's curiosity of the past. "You know, they burned the school down. Only five of us survived: me, Andu, Philipos, Kidane, and Licci." Ne'Amin spoke with his eyes to the ground, kicking the pebbles near his feet. "We were the only ones who ran when we smelled the benzene."

You have seen such horror since I left, Timneet thought. She raised her wounded hand to Ne'Amin's face, lifting his chin.

Ne'Amin continued, "I found a neighbor in Barka to lead me to the grounds out west where they would take me and train me to fight. Something told me you were on the fields, and I prayed every night that I would find you." Ne'Amin paused, inhaling deeply before continuing, "Now, I finally have. I *told* you I would some-day make you my wife," he said. His cleft chin brought butterflies to her stomach.

"I have missed you," she whispered. It was a message meant for both Ne'Amin and her departed Miriam as she rubbed the pendant of the blue dove around her neck. She was able to retrieve Miriam's necklace and kiss her goodbye when the bodies of her combat team were brought to Ne'Amin's cave after the rescue from the prison. With Ne'Amin's help Timneet had clasped Miriam's chain around her neck. She promised to never forget her sister and prayed that her soul, along with their mothers and the rest of Timneet's family, rested more peacefully than on earth.

"I have missed you, too," Ne'Amin replied, bringing his forehead to Timneet's. Back on the camp grounds of Ne'Amin's military family, they sat together on a bed of hay. A tub of water and soap sat on the ground beside their feet. Ne'Amin had used it to clean Timneet's wounds.

"What about the troublesome three sisters?" Timneet asked Ne'Amin the whereabouts of her classmates as she sat perfectly still on the bed. Timneet was still focused on piecing together the puzzle she left behind. *What happened to everyone else? Where did they all go? Above all, are they safe?*

"The regime captured and imprisoned them when they missed school the day before the fire," Ne'Amin told her. Timneet shook her head at their fate. Ne'Amin inched closer and whispered, "Before I escaped, I heard the regime maimed nearly all of their relatives and even decapitated a few. The bastards forced the girls on the streets when they were released. They're probably beggars, now. My only hope is that they are somewhere safe…and together."

"Oh, my sisters! The street is no place for girls, especially with the patrols still in the villages." Timneet bit her lower lip. The pain from her upper row of digging teeth overpowered the one burning in her chest. "Why didn't they escape?"

"I don't think they knew how or had anyone to show them the way." Ne'Amin took hold of Timneet's cold hands. "We were blessed Timneet."

"Imagine the day when we will regain our streets, Ne'Amin," she said. "Keep that in your heart, always." Timneet lightly touched his chest. His warm, inviting eyes mesmerized her, so much so that she lost the words necessary to continue in conversation.

Ne'Amin parted his lips into an endearing smile and said, "I will." He reached for her, and Timneet welcomed the embrace. It was not the first the couple shared, and it certainly would not be the last. "Timneet my sister, it's near. I can feel it inside of me."

They swayed in each other's arms. Home and the battlefield were one and the same when it came to death. The murders of their relatives, dear friends, and brothers and sisters in combat were unshakeable memories. They comforted each other, spending the night detailing every moment passed in life since the final goodbye uttered at Timneet's door and the promise of a *tomorrow*. War made the world an ugly place to live in, but the serenity in knowing she was in Ne'Amin's arms again assured Timneet that she would no longer have to face the beast alone.

Ne'Amin sang a song of freedom and ran his hand through her thick locks that she had cut short the day she entered the battlefield as a warrior woman.

> *"Eritrea, we hold you in our hearts*
> *Until the day we will unite.*
> *Eritrea, you live in our songs*
> *Forever and ever, we keep your name alive."*

Timneet longed for Ne'Amin as he sang. When he finished, she pulled back the covers for him to recline by her side, grateful for the death of solitude. Together they lay and discovered a love they were now mature enough to ignite. Several passionate nights turned to months of lying underneath shawls and rocking the hay beneath them. Their scarred bodies united feverishly, and at long last, love blossomed into life.

***

In five months time, Timneet noticed a swelling of her belly. When she came to the realization of life growing within her, an internal kick of her stomach, she darted to Ne'Amin inside the tent above their cave as he instructed a training session to newcomers.

"Ne'Amin, my brother," Timneet called, rushing to his side.

"Timneet, can this wait?" he asked sternly as he pointed to his younger students.

"No, it cannot!" she exclaimed.

Ne'Amin turned to his class and announced, "Carry on with the lesson. I'll return shortly."

Timneet took hold of his hand and led him into the cave from which she had just emerged. When they reached the bed of hay where they had slept together every day since their reunion, she sat Ne'Amin down, her heart and mind racing. The excitement of the moment would not allow her to sit still, so she stood as she squirmed like a child. A smile rushed to her lips, pouring the thrilling news.

"I've cherished every waking moment by your side, and now God has blessed us with another kind of union."

"What is it, Timneet? What is it that you are trying to tell me?" Ne'Amin asked.

"We are expecting a child," she answered, caressing her belly.

Ne'Amin looked into her eyes, blinking as though insects threatened his sight. Within a matter of seconds, he rose from their bed, buckled to his knees, and buried his face in her stomach as he wept. "Thank you, Lord. Oh, thank you, Lord. You have been so good to us."

Timneet joined his side on the ground, kneeling carefully, and rejoiced just the same.

Ne'Amin held Timneet in his arms and swayed back and forth. He then swiftly helped Timneet off the floor and led her to the bed. "Listen to me, Timneet. You are not to fight anymore, do you understand?" he ordered gently, wiping his tears. "It is far too dangerous in the fields for you while carrying a child."

Timneet nodded in agreement. "I will stay behind, cook with the other women and receive messages and orders from the informants." Timneet referred to the other women who were not on the fields because they were either wounded or carrying a child just the same.

Soon enough, the father of her child, the only love she had ever known, ran about the cave and the camping grounds above shouting the blessing that came upon their family, that they were now to be a unit of three.

"God is good," he yelled as he ran. "God is great!"

***

A wailing at the foot of the cave woke Timneet up from her slumber. It had been one month since she realized the life within her, and her stomach had grown almost twice its size. As she slowly rose from her cot at the sound of men sobbing, she was approached by Ne'Amin's combat family entering the cave with a body dangling on the back of another. They lay the body down beside Timneet and Ne'Amin's bed. The head of the slain soldier and the majority of his face was wrapped in gauze. His eyes were just as Miriam's at the time of her death—open and frightening to watch.

"Who is that?" Timneet shrieked. She attempted to sprint but the weight of her stomach only allowed for quick walking. She yelled at the foot of the cave for her husband to come down, "Ne'Amin!"

The men continued to weep over the corpse, and Timneet grew more panicked, asking, "Does Ne'Amin know that you've brought someone here? Who is he?" she squealed, thinking of the poor man's family. She thought of her brother, Amaniel. How would she know if he ever claimed the same fate on the field. *Would* she ever know?

"Timneet," Ne'Amin's good friend, Alazar, came to her side and gently took her by the arm back to the bed.

"You need to get Ne'Amin," she whispered. In addition to teaching, Ne'Amin was in charge of praying over their casualties before the burial ceremonies. He was the most religious of them all, speaking of God's wish for Eritrea to be free and peace to come across their land.

"Timneet," Alazar wailed. Before he could finish, the men huddled around the slain soldier began their mourning again, lamenting on each other's shoulders.

"Ne'Amin, our brother…"

"How can we do this without you?"

"Ne'Amin, our sweet, sweet brother…"

"Where do we go from here?"

"Ne'Amin…"

"What?" Timneet rose from her bed. "What are you saying?" she shouted and shoved the men with all her might clear of her way to get through to the body on the floor. "Ne'Amin? Ne'Amin?" Timneet screamed until her lungs had no more to give. Her knees gave way and she dropped to the ground, showing no sign that the strike had physically harmed her. Instead, she rolled onto her side, gasping for air as she wept, putting her arm around Ne'Amin's waist. She latched on to him as though the more she squeezed the better her chances of bringing him back.

Timneet heard the other women, her companions in pregnancy, usher the soldiers out of the area designated for Ne'Amin and Timneet, where they lay their heads every night. They had privacy again, like the night before, when he told her he wanted nothing more than to make her the happiest wife to have ever lived.

"How could you leave me to do this on my own?" she whimpered. "Why would you do this to us? After everything—everything we've been through. Why didn't you keep yourself safe, right here with me? Why didn't I make you stay off the fields like you made me? Is your presence in our child's life not as important as mine? Why, Ne'Amin? Why?"

Timneet lay on the floor of the cave in the same position clinging onto Ne'Amin for two days before their brothers and sisters removed his body for burial.

***

One month of mourning later, Timneet arranged a plan for the future of her child. "When can I leave?" Timneet whispered to the two women taking turns, stirring a large pot of porridge on open flames.

"Timneet, are you really going to do this?" the younger one, Alganesh asked, expecting a child herself.

"Yes," Timneet hissed. "Ne'Amin's family deserves to have and raise his child."

Timneet kept her voice down. Freedom fighters strolled about the tents, close friends of Ne'Amin, who would try to forbid her from leaving. Avoiding that was simple as long as the women who knew of her plan kept their vow of secrecy.

"We're not arguing *that*. We know that these children with no fathers or mothers, most with both parents on the fields, need to be raised by the father's family. No spat there," Abeba, the older one, confirmed.

"Well then, if you know that, what is the problem?"

"Timneet, you can't be serious. You are ready to *burst*. Look at you—at least seven months pregnant, and you want an informant to drop you off in Barka? Just like that? Have you gone mad? They'll recognize and snatch you. You know there are messengers meant for this—for bringing children to the father's family. You, yourself, don't have to go," Abeba shared her words of wisdom. According to Ne'Amin, Abeba had been in battle since the very beginning of the war. She knew how things worked, especially since her back injury confined her to the camping grounds where she worked heavily with informants. She had been shot several times by the enemy, but miraculously she survived and could still walk, albeit at the pace of a snail.

"Nonsense, I'm having this child in Barka and *in* Ne'Amin's home, and then I'll visit my grandmother in Zigib before I come back."

"Timneet, didn't you hear about Zigib?" Alganesh asked.

"What?" Timneet asked, alarmed. "Tell me what you know."

"Zigib doesn't exist anymore. They say that they've moved everyone to Unah," the young soldier revealed.

"Unah, but why? That's so far away!" Timneet exclaimed.

"I don't know. My sister Samrawit lives near Zigib and she sent a message through that informant, Rahwa, who told us that shockingly, there were no deaths but that the homes were destroyed and all villagers were taken to Unah. She mentioned that they bussed them there," Alganesh shared.

"Who is *they*? The regime?" Timneet asked.

"Yes," Alganesh replied, lowering her head.

"When will Rahwa be here next?" Timneet asked the seasoned soldier. The urgency in Timneet's voice was conveyed through a high pitched tone.

"She will be here this Friday," Abeba replied, patting Timneet on the back.

"Well, then Friday it is. Thank you sisters for the information." Timneet headed for the cave where she planned on preparing for her four day trip with an informant to Barka.

***

Timneet remembered what it felt like to knock on the green arch door years before when Ne'Amin's mother, Mama Birikhti, would stand on the other side asking who it was in her sing-song voice as if she really did not know. For a moment, Timneet felt what it was to be a young girl, one whose heart had been stolen by a boy at such a tender age.

The thought of being in Ne'Amin's home without him by her side became unbearable for her once she arrived. In front of his door, she relived her many days spent with Ne'Amin years prior. She longed for him, and it grew increasingly painful the longer she stood on the steps, bracing herself before knocking, for Ne'Amin's mother to meet her at the door. At a moment's notice, her energy drained from her body, and the misfortune of an unlucky life swarmed her swollen body, until she fell onto the steps of his home and wept with all of her might. Timneet had no care in the world for who heard her cries.

A woman angrily flung open the door, investigating the sounds of the night that invaded the private silence of her home. The woman yelled at empty space meeting the level of her eye, until she realized Timneet lying on the floor.

"What are you doing?" the woman barked.

The language the woman spoke forced every single hair on Timneet's body to rise. Timneet looked up at the woman and squirmed. This was not the face of the mother she had longed for—*this* was the face of an irate, Ethiopian woman.

I'm finished, Timneet thought.

Timneet's legs trembled, beads of sweat surfaced on her forehead and behind her ears. She lay on the floor, and choked on her words as she tried to explain. "I am sorry." Timneet forced the words in Amharic. "I am terribly mistaken. There was a family who lived here." She cleverly decided not to disclose the name of the Eritrean family.

"Here get up from the floor," the woman urged, helping a rather heavy Timneet to her feet. "Which family are you looking for?" the woman questioned, intrigued. "I have lived here for years and can direct you. What is your name, child?" the woman asked.

"I apologize for disrupting your evening. I meant no harm," Timneet replied, avoiding the woman's question and eyes, eager to escape. There were plenty of Ethiopian spies who lived among Eritreans, and although this woman seemed caring, Timneet opted not to take a chance.

Timneet turned her back to the woman, her hands trembling as though she was holding a heap of ice, preparing to walk down the hill from where she came. All at once, four Ethiopian patrols turned the corner and began their ascent. By the way each of them struck their batons to their own hands, they were clearly in search of a few troublemakers in the area.

Timneet shook violently as she whipped back around facing the woman, grabbing onto her arms with eyes as wide as could be. She looked to her swollen belly and back again at the woman while the men drew closer.

"We'll hang anyone involved," shouted a patrol.

"We must find their homes and do it there. No more street killings. The families do not hurt as much as when the bodies are left in their homes," the other soldier chimed in, planning the rest of their evening.

Timneet silently pled for the impossible to become reality from a woman who shared *their* blood.

The soldiers were now at the level of the woman's home and one of the militants removed the beret from his head and lifted it to the woman. She nodded her head and offered a crooked smile. Timneet was innocent by association—an Ethiopian woman and the pitch dark of the night saved her.

The woman turned to Timneet, and in Amharic, she purposely spoke loudly enough for the regime to hear. "Come in my sweet sister, it's so cold out here!" she yelled, taking Timneet into her home.

"You could have been killed!" the woman expressed as soon as she locked the door behind her.

"I—I—I," Timneet stood in a home celebrated with the Ethiopian flag. She had never stepped foot in an Ethiopian home, much less spoken to one who was not a member of the regime.

What just happened? An act of heroism or a cruel joke? An Ethiopian saving the life of an Eritrean—I am not alive. I am not witnessing this. It is unheard of! Timneet screamed within. She began to speak to the woman instead of battling her own thoughts. "Why did you help me?" she asked, astonished that words were successfully leaving her mouth and making sense.

"I wasn't going to simply let you die," the woman replied. "For what? What did you do to deserve what they would have done to you had they known who you were? You may have fooled those imbeciles, but I could tell you are Eritrean."

"I do not know what to say."

"Do not let the regime control you, child. They've taught you hate, haven't they? Not everyone is a member of the regime. *They* don't equal Ethiopia. *They* equal hate. Ethiopia and its people, we do not *all* possess hatred in our hearts for Eritreans. I hope I taught you that tonight. No need to even speak. What is done is done. Thank the Almighty that you did not knock on anyone else's door on this hill. Your fate would have been far different. And, when you thank Him, thank him for Mihret. That is my name," she said. Mihret caressed Timneet's arms. "You must be cold...and hungry," she added.

"Yes, I am," Timneet responded, "but if you do not have anything to eat, I understand."

"Nonsense, that is no discussion to have." Mihret stopped guiding Timneet through her cozy home and said, "I did not catch your name, child."

"My name is Timneet."

"Come, have a seat." Mihret aided Timneet to sit on the couch, outstretching her arms for Timneet to hold onto. "Bend your knees, lower your bottom. There you have it." Mihret placed a pillow behind Timneet's back for comfort.

"I have not sat down much throughout my pregnancy," Timneet explained.

Mihret had already scurried to the kitchen to prepare a meal.

Timneet surveyed the room. Two black and white photographs of young men hung low on Mihret's walls, and on a table directly in front of the framed pictures, lit candles exposed their faces.

Mihret returned with *injera* and lamb's meat to go along with the bread on a silver platter then sat beside Timneet, offering to feed her. "Here my child, you must be starving."

Timneet had not eaten good food in the past five years. She had grown tired of the porridge on the fields. She devoured the entire plate well within a matter of minutes, taking bites from Mihret's hands and from her own, forgetting to ask Mihret her kinship to the men on the wall.

"You poor child," Mihret repeated as Timneet finished.

"I blame my womb. I am not normally this rude. Please forgive me."

"I am only poking fun, Timneet."

"Ne'Amin teased me all the time about my love for food," Timneet recalled aloud, fighting back tears.

"Who is Ne'Amin?"

"My—my—," Timneet's airway refused to let her lungs receive. "My—my—child's father." Timneet swallowed hastily.

"Calm your soul, my child. Breathe." Mihret rubbed Timneet's back gently. "We can discuss other things."

Timneet continued, determined to find the answers she was seeking. "Mihret, there was a family who lived here—right here in this home. I know—I was here a handful of times after school."

"Is that why you came? To find them? Child, do you know you are risking your life? *And* your child's?" Mihret pointed vigorously to Timneet's stomach.

Timneet ignored the questions and continued. "They must have been the dwellers of this home before you. My child's father, Ne'Amin, his family lived here when we were younger."

"Oh, dear." Mihret grabbed hold of her cheeks. Her eye twitched as she responded, "Timneet, how do I say this?" Another pause built an unwanted anticipation. "From what I know," Mihret pointed to herself, "each member of that family was beaten and tortured to death when their son escaped. Could their son be the man you speak of? Did Ne'Amin escape? Is that why you came?To find him and his family?"

The room spun and although seated with feet planted firmly, the unsteadiness refused to subside. *What am I to do now?* Timneet thought, panic growing within her.

"Speak to me. Let it out," Mihret pled.

"My child's father was killed in a missile strike. And now, his family has wasted away, too. I wanted to share with his parents that although Ne'Amin was killed, they would have a grandchild to look after—a little reminder of Ne'Amin," she wailed.

"Oh, Timneet." Mihret grabbed Timneet's head and placed it on her chest, sharing the pain of her tears.

***

On their second morning together, Timneet and Mihret sat for a breakfast of *ga'at*, a rich, doughy favorite of Timneet's and every pregnant woman, complemented by the *berbere* spice and yogurt.

"I will be heading to my grandmother's soon. I have decided Adey will raise my child. I need your help, though, Mihret." Timneet confided in Mihret, trusting her wholly. Her plan was brewing, but guidance was most important.

"You have my word," Mihret responded, confidently. "Anything you need."

"I know you have far exceeded the good deeds the Lord has asked of you, but I ask that you help me with this."

"Timneet, what is it that you need? Come out and tell me, already."

"I need a messenger to deliver a note to Adey. I believe she is in Unah, but I don't know where. I want her to be prepared for my arrival and plan on giving her a message to tell her when we can meet, so she can take me back to her home. She is an old woman. If I am not careful I can make her leave this Earth earlier than intended. You understand I cannot simply present myself after all of these years *and* in this state," she explained. Timneet pressed her dress under her navel further accentuating her bump. "Her soul would surely depart from shock."

"I have just the person you are seeking!" Mihret exclaimed. "She is a fifty-year-old woman imprisoned in a nine-year-old shell," she declared, pointing her upright finger in the air.

"A nine-year-old girl?" Timneet laughed. "Mihret, my sister, I mean no disrespect, but I am trying to send a note to Adey, not get myself and my child murdered. The girl may scream if I do not include a sugar-filled treat and then what? She could lead the regime right *to* me!"

"Oh stop, it isn't like that at all." Mihret tapped Timneet's shoulder. Neither of them had touched their breakfast, getting lost in planning. "The child's mother manages a courier route and hires the least suspecting members of her family—her children. Is that not shrewd?" Mihret cackled.

Timneet's uneasiness showed. "Are you confident in the child's work?" she asked.

Since Timneet's escape, young children dominated the mail carrier roles, delivering secret letters to family members throughout Eritrea as a form of communication.

"Absolutely! I have met the child. She is extraordinary, and of all the child couriers, she is the most disciplined. She listens to her mother, and more importantly, she adheres to rules. Her mother will find your grandmother for you, and all we would have to do is get the letter to her daughter," Mihret explained.

"What is her name? What does she look like?" Timneet asked.

"Her name is Sophia. She wears two braids, split down the middle. I am telling you Timneet, the child listens. Her mother has trained her to leave one second before the agreed upon appointment time between her mother and the sender."

"This sounds promising."

"Trust in me and this family I am presenting you with," Mihret boasted of her connections. "They are legitimate. I only wish there was a way Sophia could deliver a note to your grandmother without us having to go ourselves—it's dangerous between here and Unah, patrols hidden throughout the villages in between—but the mother and child only send messages from people they meet in person. It is a trust issue, my child. Heaven forbid Sophia is snatched by the regime like the other girls who write notes for senders they have never met, messages sent through friends of friends—the girls always end up delivering to an address that is occupied by the regime in a setup."

"Oh, dear! No, I will go myself, then. Where would I meet her?"

"You foolish girl! You are not to leave this home! I will deliver the letter for you," Mihret announced.

"Have you lost your mind, sister? I would rather flaunt my sought after face in front of the regime than have you risk your life. It is entirely too dangerous for us to walk together in these streets. The regime will take one look at us, a known resident with a stranger on her arm, and they'll immediately suspect *you* of wrongdoing."

"Nonsense, Timneet! Had I known you would have insisted on something this foolish, I would not have suggested such a plan. Our time together *has* been short, but I still look at you as one of my own," Mihret exclaimed, pouting.

Timneet recalled the young men in the photos on Mihret's wall. Over the last few days it had dawned on her that the candles may have been lit in mourning. *What if they're her sons? What if now, she has none of her own children? All that she has done for me— saving my life, offering me shelter and food, and a plan to bring me and Adey together again, all in a matter of two days—it makes sense that the love she has showered me with comes from a yearning to turn back time and give her children the same.*

Timneet's thoughts grew distracted by Mihret's argument that she would deliver the letter. The valid points shared between them ensued for another hour before Mihret finally agreed.

"You are lucky that I should concede in a dispute like this. My head is pounding and that is the only reason I let you win." Mihret rubbed the back of her hand across her forehead.

"Say what you will," Timneet said, grinning at her success. "I would never allow you to risk your life again." She embraced Mihret. "Where would I meet the child?"

"At the marketplace in Unah, next to the tallest church in all the region. I can arrange for my cousin, Girmai, to meet you shortly after you've given Sophia the letter. I'll give him a quick call from the phone at the corner store and give him the signal to expect you. He will take you to his home, and Sophia will meet you at Girmai's one to two days later, with your grandmother. I would ask Girmai to deliver the message for you but much like Sophia he's been scarred by the regime robbing him of his friends who have gone missing while helping others. He is already running a huge risk keeping fugitives in his home. If your grandmother is too ill to make the journey, then we will have you meet somewhere closer to her home. Is that fair?"

"Very well." Timneet clapped her hands onto her lap. "Set the appointment for one week from today, next Sunday. That will give me enough time to make it to Unah."

Excited, Timneet kissed Mihret on the cheek and set out to write the message to her grandmother, wobbling swiftly into the bedroom.

"Aren't you going to eat the *ga'at* I prepared for you, my child?" asked Mihret.

"I will be back shortly, Mihret!" Timneet exclaimed. She moved to the next room and eased her rear into the chair at the foot of their shared bed, pen and paper in hand, as love and hope poured through her scribbling hand.

***

"And a very good morning to you, as well." Timneet blessed the birds chirping outside the small bedroom window the morning after Mihret offered her a plan to see Adey again. Peace was in the air.

Cautious not to awaken Mihret, Timneet rolled onto the floor from the outside of the bed. Timneet insisted on sleeping on top of the covers. It was perfect for the escapes to the bathroom which occurred several times throughout the night.

Timneet entered the bathroom and dissected her face in the mirror. She was one step closer to finding resolve in her heart. She was less than a week away from reuniting with her beloved grandmother. *She'll be thrilled to see me,* Timneet thought. "Adey will be much more excited to see you," she cooed to her belly.

"Wonderful, you have already awoken," Mihret announced as Timneet made her way back into the bedroom. "We must get you prepared," Mihret said, springing from the bed and into the closet. She revealed her sewing machine and kit.

"Well, aren't you rich?" Timneet marveled. She had not seen a sewing apparatus or even come close to the magical machine in Mihret's hands since visiting her mother at her seamstress job for the regime long ago.

"I have finally finished your disguise, the perfect camouflage."

"What is it?" Timneet pressed. She clutched the long black torn fabric at its other end while Mihret rocked the material from side to side, gleefully. "I haven't the slightest idea why you are so giddy."

"Think, Timneet," Mihret urged, raising her finger to her temple. "Think! Sophia knows you will be at the market by dawn, which so happens to be when both Muslims and Christians head to the mosque and church for morning devotion. If you are running behind, you will know—you will see a majority of Christians. This simply means you must quicken your pace." Mihret raised her eyebrows. "Now, guess who will be a Muslim wife beginning tomorrow?"

"You are a star, my sister!" It was the disguise that would allow Timneet to walk through the villages unbothered and reach the marketplace where Sophia would be waiting. The patrols did not interfere with morning prayer or the hike to reach the sanctuaries. The devout were untouchable.

"I am thrilled you agree! I want you to try it on, and we'll see if any changes need to be made. Here, come near the window. There is more light there." Mihret measured Timneet while Timneet stood on a small stool. She left more room in the front of her gown so as to deflect any attention to her stomach. Mihret hurried to her seat and began fiddling with the machine immediately. There was no time to waste.

"Mihret, be careful with your fingers," Timneet warned.

"Oh, I will be just fine. The faster I finish any corrections that need to be made, the more time we will have to share before you leave me."

"I have told you hundreds of times," Timneet reassured her dear friend, "I will be back before I head to the fields again. I want Adey to have this child, now that Ne'Amin's relatives are not here to take care of him or her."

"To the living room, child." Mihret helped Timneet dismount the stool and gave Timneet her arm. Timneet leaned on her during their walk into the next room.

Mihret pinned needles along Timneet's back and cautiously twirled her around to face the wall.

"Mihret, my sister, who are those men?" Timneet asked, pointing to the wall directly in front of her. Timneet had not asked in the few days she had inhabited Mihret's home because of her suspicion that the men had perished, but curiosity nudged her one too many times to remain silent.

Mihret remained quiet and still.

After a few minutes of silence, Timneet whispered, "I apologize. Forgive me, Mihret." The subject matter was clearly sensitive.

"They were my sons." Mihret continued, the regime murdered them in front of my husband."

"Oh, Mihret! I'm so sorry! Why? But, you're Ethiopian, too! Where is your husband now?"

"Merlus and Gedaw were murdered because they refused to serve." Mihret sat on the chair against the wall decorated with her sons' faces. "We raised them to respect Ethiopians and Eritreans the same, even with hatred everywhere around us."

"You and your husband are admirable people. I have learned so much from you," Timneet said. She descended from the stool and held Mihret's hands.

"My husband, Tirfu? Do not admire *him*," Mihret replied, fuming. She referred to her absent partner, the man with no picture in their home to his name. "The coward hung himself the day they shot our boys, leaving me to bury our only children and cope with a pain that can only be washed away in heaven." Mihret hugged herself tightly, twisting her back from side to side. "He left me to find all three of their bodies breathless—the bastard."

***

The following morning, Timneet dressed as quickly as her expectant body would allow.

Today is the day, she thought. Mihret walked into the bedroom as Timneet struggled with the back of the gown. Mihret stood nose to nose with Timneet, resting her hands on Timneet's shoulders.

"Keep still and keep calm. You are so eager to leave me, is that it?" Mihret questioned playfully as she fixed Timneet's garb. She rubbed Timneet's stomach with her permission, lowering her stance and talking to her belly. "Are you rushing your mother?"

"No, I only want to be on time. That is all, my sister."

The two had grown quite fond of each other. The company they shared was full of laughs. Mihret wrapped Timneet's hair and face with the gown's attached black scarf. They sat for a cup of tea and bread, until it was time for Timneet to begin her journey toward Sophia. Mihret insisted once more in desperation when they reached the front door, "Are you certain you want to do this? I can still go for you."

"No, my sister. You have done plenty already. If they were to capture you, I do not know what I would do with myself. Mihret, I will be fine. Remember, I will return." Timneet smiled through her eyes, attempting to restore comfort in the heart of her dear friend.

Timneet leaned on the closed front door of Mihret's home with one hand and embraced Mihret with the other.

"Remember, Sophia has two braids. Her school bag will differ from the rest. Look for the red fabric sewn on her sack—the one that looks as though it's been dipped in goat's blood." Mihret beamed and said, "I patched it on there for her myself. If you are a second late, she will leave. She *will*, Timneet. Please be on time."

Mihret turned the doorknob, tears falling from her eyes, before she exclaimed, "Silly child, you almost forgot your letter!" Mihret ran into the bedroom and seized the note from under the pillow.

"Mihret, you truly are my star. You saved me a trip back to the house." Timneet pressed the almost forgotten letter onto her chest.

Before opening the door, Timneet expressed, "I want my child to be born with the same love as you have for others. If it is a girl," Timneet prepared for the thrill in Mihret's voice, "I will name her after you, my sister."

"No, no," Mihret replied, shutting her eyes and shaking her head. "Haven't you heard it is bad luck to name a daughter after someone you know, Timneet?"

"Why?" Timneet questioned.

"You only do that with male children. A son can even be named after his own father."

"I have never heard of such a thing. Besides, I am not one to follow rules," Timneet shared.

"Now, now," Mihret appeased Timneet. "If it is a boy, well I think you know what to do there." Mihret smiled. "You should name him after Ne'Amin. If it is a girl, name her something meaningful, like Equality. In the end, is that not what you all will have fought for—equality and freedom."

"I adore those names, Mihret! Ma'arinet or Natsinet. Help me decide, my sister."

"Let your heart decide." She patted Timneet's chest.

"Thank you for everything, my sister."

"Best wishes to you, and Timneet," Mihret struggled with her last words, "please, be safe."

Timneet left Mihret's home and melded with the downhill marching crowd of civilians. The patrols walked in pairs along the bottom of the hills.

We are all created equal in the eyes of the Lord. We bleed red just like you. We are your equals, and you have no right to treat us anything less than such. We are human beings and we deserve the respect and honor owed to all of the Lord's children. And yet, you have lost the message of our God. Where is the equality? Where is your obedience to the Lord? Timneet stared at the forming queue of patrols as she descended the hill. The security of the Lord and Ne'Amin's presence was incredibly strong.

I think I've just answered my own question, she thought. *If the Lord wishes a daughter unto me, I will give her the honorable name of Equality—my princess, Ma'arinet.*

Timneet could feel Mihret's eyes on her back as she walked farther away.

Forward. Keep forward, she repeatedly reminded herself for the sake of sanity. The words guided her every move until she reached the market, five days later and a few villages in distance, where Sophia the courier and the village of Unah awaited her arrival.

CHAPTER 9

Narrated by Ma'arinet Neguse

Clouds come floating into my life,
no longer to carry rain or usher storm,
but to add color to my sunset sky.
—Rabindranath Tagore

Director Almaz flicked the tears from her face with her forefingers. She raised her head from the letter whispering its last few lines, "May time speed to bring me near you again. May our love ease the pain of the past."

She stood near the window, overlooking what sounded like the busiest street of the morning, filled with a goat herder yelling at his flock and a crowd of frenzied civilians running from a loose cow.

"Director, have you seen this letter before? Did you know the woman who wrote it?" The words she had read from my mother's barely legible letter leapt from her mouth in a quivering voice and shook me to my core. My heart raced faster than my thoughts. Despite the firm lock of my feet to the ground, my legs quaked violently. "Director, please answer me," I urged.

She faced us again, as pale as her uniform, and I grew more concerned with her fainting and dying right in front of us prior to getting any answers. It was selfish of me, I know.

Aunt Kibra interjected the silence, "She needs to know what you know!" She held onto my hand for support. I sunk farther into the folding chair while my aunt maintained the same tenacity she had with Zahara downstairs.

Director Almaz continued to ignore us. The distance between her eyebrows and the tip of her nose lessened as she crinkled her face in confusion. She struggled with unauthorized noises escaping from her throat, wincing as though humiliated by them until she finally garnered sensible words. The director walked back to her desk as though she were trudging through mud. She found her seat again, nearly missing it for the second time since we had met. "I thought you died in the attack on the orphanage," she revealed, covering her mouth with the tips of her fingers. "I thought I broke my vow to your mother." She stared into the space between our shoulders then looked directly into my eyes. "My," she whispered, seemingly in disbelief, "you look just like her."

"You," I held my pounding head, "you, knew my mother?" I was losing my breath. The four walls around us were closing in. I shut my eyes and lived the next few moments in darkness.

"I was with her on the last day of her life—the day you were born."

"She died on my birthday? You're certain?"

"Child," the Director assured me, "I found your mother at the market surrounded by beggars ready to give birth to you on the floor."

"My mother was a beggar?" My chest elevated and collapsed frantically.

"Tell her everything, Director Almaz. This child has been without answers for far too long," my aunt shared, highlighting the desperation and tightening her grip on my hand.

I prepared for and fully accepted the worst possible truth to be mine. Anything was better than not having a story at all.

"Her name was Timneet."

"Oh, God." It was becoming more real. My navel shot to my spine forcing nausea to meet the back of my throat.

The director's voice deepened, changing the air of the room. "I found your mother at the marketplace while on my way to work over twenty years ago." Director Almaz began retelling the accounts of the eventful day while I imagined my mother on the street, pregnant and helpless. I had never put an image to the day of my birth, and the thought that it would be as painful a sight as the director described brought a deep sadness to my heart.

Director Almaz went on, "We used a market worker's wheelbarrow to transport her to the hospital."

"How did she get to the market?"

"Ma'arinet, before your mother passed on the table, there were times when she held minutes of conversation with me between her contractions. Her hope was for me to tell you everything she relayed to me. I cannot believe I am actually doing it!" she shrieked.

I was anxious to get the information. *Do not yell at this woman,* I persuaded myself. "Director Almaz, please. What did she tell you?" *Focus!* I wanted to scream at her.

"I held her secrets in my heart for all these years, not even revealing to my closest friends where this mysterious woman came from, or who she was. Your mother, Timneet, was a soldier and her face was wanted by many patrols. When Timneet made the decision to give birth in the village and have you raised by your father's family, she found informants to smuggle her back. Only when she arrived to your father's home, she learned that all of them had been..." The director raised her head to the ceiling and mumbled a few words.

They were killed. The frown on the director's face and the multiple signs of the cross she made revealed the fate of my father's family.

Director Almaz continued, "Your father was a soldier who passed in the war."

"What was his name?" I pled.

The director paused, looking for it in the severely faded message. "Ah, yes. Two letters in his name are missing, so you would have never known from this letter, but it *is* here," she said, pointing and squinting. "It was Ne'Amin." She repeated with more confidence of her memory, "Yes, yes it was Ne'Amin."

"What else did she tell you, Director Almaz?"

"She had a few requests she asked me to fulfill in the event she passed. I think her body was telling her she was not going to survive," the director recalled, "but that certainly did not stop her from trying."

"Go on," I urged. I was nearly begging to hear my mother's final bits of conversation, hanging on the director's every word.

"Timneet first asked that this letter would go wherever you went. Maybe she knew the woman you would become and the persistence you would have in finding someone who had read it before. Timneet was a very wise woman." Director Almaz upheld her chin in the web of her hand, her elbows resting on her messy desk, seemingly mesmerized by a mother's intuition. She continued, "Timneet also asked that she would be buried and her body not be given to the regime. She was asking me to risk my job and furthermore, my life." The director pressed her hands to her chest.

My aunt explained, "Back then, hospital staff were ordered to yield the bodies of the dead, and if a doctor, nurse, or aide hid a body, especially that of a freedom fighter, their fate was death by hanging in front of their family and the public."

I disregarded any talk of reason. After all, this was my *mother*. "Did you bury her?" I asked.

My aunt sensed my oncoming anger and squeezed my hand. If

she believed it would calm me down, it worked, but only for a few seconds.

Director Almaz alternated her attention between my aunt and me. "I risked it all for a woman I did not even know. Her spirit was so kind and she fought for us to be free. How could I not obey her wish?"

"Where is she buried?" I asked. I was moments away from grabbing my aunt's hand, springing from my seat, and running to my mother's grave.

"I buried her just outside. I put her necklace over her grave and luckily, the regime never found it. Over the years, I made it my job to clean and take great care of her necklace so that it stayed beautiful. Come, let me show you, child."

I'm going to meet my mother, the realization settled. *Finally, the closure I've been desperately seeking all these years!*

Aunt Kibra pulled me into her arms as we rose from our seats. "I told you we were close!" she exclaimed.

We walked down the stairs and a moment from the office stuck me like a wrecking ball.

"Director," I paused in my step, "you said you thought you broke your promise to my mother." I waited until she turned around slowly. "What was your vow?"

"Ma'arinet…child, Timneet wanted you to know her story and learn of the woman she was. Her hope for you, her *timneet,* was for you to be a better woman, more powerful and wiser than she. Timneet wanted you to know all of this, that this was her wish for you."

"Thank you, Director Almaz," I heard my aunt express on my behalf.

All I could offer were half-nods, a frown, and eyes that swelled with liquid pain. *I wish she were here,* I thought.

As if she heard my yearning desire, Director Almaz urged, "Let me take you to her."

We reached the waiting area before exiting. Zahara was occupied announcing names. Director Almaz hurried Aunt Kibra and I outdoors through an exit meant for hospital staff. It felt as though the air thickened with each step I took, making it harder for me to breathe. I trailed Director Almaz and Aunt Kibra, persuading myself to believe in the moment—that what I was experiencing was real. The questions would not cease, though. *Am I really about to meet my mother? What do I do once I see her grave? Would it be weird to them if I talked to her? I wonder if I'm anything like her. Would Director Almaz even know if I asked?*

Director Almaz led us to the back door of the maternity wing where a small garden bloomed with sunflowers. We moved in closer, and as the director silently pointed in its direction turning to look back at me, I nearly fell to my knees.

I stood there, my feet refusing to move forward. *She's underground. This is it. She's been reduced to dirt and time eating her away into nothingness. She deserved so much more. I deserved so much more.*

Aunt Kibra stood as still as I. Director Almaz walked past her, took me by my hands, and brought me near the largest sunflower, the one which shone the brightest. It was adorned with a necklace, a gorgeous pendant of a blue dove on a chain, around the base of its stalk.

I approached my mother's grave with the timid walk of a child fearing her parent. Not wanting to stand directly on the soil that covered her, I kept a short distance. My fingers tingled, every strand of hair on my body rising. My shoulders met my ears in tension as I folded my arms above my stomach, trying to make sense of it all. *How fair is it that she died and I lived?* I thought.

I collapsed onto my mother's grave, weeping. I wept for the mother I never knew and the relationship I wished I had. I cried for her pain on the day she gave her life so I could live mine.

Director Almaz ran to my side, kneeling beside me as I lay sprawled on my mother's grave sobbing. She turned me over onto my back and lifted my head onto her thigh. She took the necklace from the sunflower and clasped it around my neck.

"She's with you always, Ma'arinet…and she always has been," the director shared, caressing my hair. Aunt Kibra met us on the soil seconds later, gripping my hand in hers.

I opened my eyes. Through the blur my tears had formed, the sun was bright as could be, beaming on my face.

"Can I please have a moment to myself?" I asked of my aunt and Director Almaz. They both agreed, vigorously nodding their heads. They stood against the maternity ward back exit and watched. I turned back to her resting place and hugged the soil beneath me, realizing that she had been with me all along. When I finally decided to leave Esak, it was God's hand that placed her, in the form of courage, inside of me to do so. When I lost my babies, the Lord blessed me with her spirit guiding my faith and making me a stronger believer in a brighter future for myself. When I was at rock bottom, my mother was with me. Every step I took, she was there. Her name was courage, and it was faith—her name was hope.

Her name was Timneet.

***

A few weeks after discovering the truth behind my birth story, I decided it was finally time for me to go home. Leaving Aunt Kibra was especially difficult as she took care of me every day since I had arrived, and in the end, she saw to it that my heart's deepest sorrow was no longer. She cried like a baby the morning of my departure, and I bawled just as hard. We had been through so much in the two months we had spent together, and the bond we shared brought serenity to my soul.

As I carried my bags to the front door, Aunt Kibra's daughter, Natsa raced to my side.

"What is it, Natsa?"

She motioned for me to come closer with her index finger and meet her at her level. I bent over and let her whisper in my ear. "I had a dream about you yesterday," she said.

"About what?" I whispered back.

"You were wearing a graduation cap and holding flowers. Do you know what that means?"

I shook my head.

"The cap means good things, like you're going to be happy, with a beautiful life and money," Natsa said.

"What do the flowers mean?" I was intrigued. I didn't know I had a dream interpreter in the family.

Natsa stepped back and ballooned her shirt. My eyes grew wide. I fought back laughs, grabbing her hands gently so her mother wouldn't see from the front door. Aunt Kibra was waiting with my other cousin, Michael, looking to hail a cab. Luckily, their backs were turned during Natsa's display.

"What does that mean?" I asked calmly, not wanting to alarm her.

"Babies!" she squealed.

I laughed so hard. "But Natsa, what about a husband?" I asked.

She twisted her wrists, her palms facing the skies, and shrugged her shoulders. "I guess that means he's coming?"

Children, I thought. How I wished I could go back to the days when I could say anything and people would excuse *me* for being a child and dreamed of being in *my* place.

I took hold of Natsa's hand and met Aunt Kibra and Michael at the front door, leaving my luggage behind in the small living area. I didn't want to waste anymore time lugging them around. I wanted to spend my last few minutes with my family.

***

Welcome to Flughafen Frankfurt. Good afternoon passengers. This is the pre-boarding announcement for flight 1116 to Chicago. We are now inviting those passengers with small children…

I stood in a lengthy line directly behind a blonde woman who must have been over six feet tall even in flats. I tapped her on her sleeveless arm and asked with an unsure smile, "Pardon, do you mind if I go ahead of you? My flight was just announced." I pointed to the glass ceiling as though the voices from the airport loudspeakers were coming from the skies above.

The woman looked down and gave me a blank stare. "I *no* understand," she replied in a thick German accent and a frown that suggested she was unwilling to even try.

I replied with the only German word I knew, "Danke."

The woman returned her attention to the front of the security check point, snubbing my effort to relate.

Even if I had managed to bypass the cold giant, there were at least one hundred passengers ahead of me. Trying was pointless and by the looks of the crowd in queue I would have had to be a linguistic expert to even say hello, much less convey a plea. At the rate the line was moving, it was clear that I would never make my flight.

Reactions are choices, I told myself. *You can choose to be angry at what was not, or you can choose to be happy at what will be because it was not. Just let go,* I thought. I heard the three simple words softly spoken in my head like the soothing sounds of wind between sheets attached to clothespins on a breezy afternoon.

"Maybe I'm just not meant to make this flight," I muttered, less philosophical than the words parading in my head.

I had nowhere to be at a designated date or time, no job to report to upon my arrival back home, no meetings to attend. Instead, I was left with all the thoughts in the world and countless pictures to sort through and piece together from the last two months of my life in an album that I would someday be able to share with my children. I readjusted the strap of my camera around my neck. *You are so good to me,* I crooned to my *picture box,* as the ladies on King Drive called it.

I set the strap apart from my mother's necklace, rubbing the blue dove between my fingers. *I will always have you near,* I thought. My mother's presence was alive in my heart, and I could feel the change inside of me. There was a power, an energy so strong, and at times, it moved me to tears. My soul was smiling again.

I turned to the line behind me in an attempt to make myself feel better about the ridiculousness of a crowd before me, and sure enough the line was just as insanely long as the one ahead. The woman behind me clung onto her slipping, empty stroller with one hand, and a luggage cart filled with two large duffle bags with her other hand. On her left ring finger was an unmistakable lustrous rock and band, and I could not help but wonder during her struggle, *Where is your husband?*

Her son, who would not keep still, had a face covered entirely with curly locks, initially, until he shook his hair out of the way and exposed his pudgy cheeks. He grew increasingly louder as he made motorcycle and truck noises, careening his plastic toys around airport pillars along the security checkpoint, until he chucked his toy cowboy onto my heel.

"Adam!" his mother shrieked.

"I am so sorry," she apologized. "Adam, come here...now." She gave her son one look, the deathly stares my mother shot at me while growing up, and the boy jumped to his feet, meeting his mother's hips at once.

She kneeled down to meet the boy at eye level and held him by his tiny fingers, whispering lovingly in his ear and patting his behind.

The German woman ahead of me had moved a considerable distance and I walked closer to her, closing the gap I had created while paying attention to the mother and son.

Adam rubbed his motorcycle and toy cowboy between his clasped hands and approached me. Through pouted lips, he said, "I'm *sahwee*. It was a ac-ci-dent."

I knelt by his side as I had seen his mother do. "*Aww*, it's okay. Don't feel bad," I said. "I'm not upset."

He buried his face in the crease of his arm, drying his tears of guilt.

I chatted with Adam as we inched closer to the machinery of airport security. Having not been around children his age in a long time, I explored the mind of a five-year-old.

"Do you know what I wanna be when I'm grown up?" Adam did not wait for my response. "The *pwime ministuh*."

"Of what country?" I asked, amused.

"*Denmahk*," Adam replied. His whole face was one huge grin.

"Denmark! Is that where you're from?"

"Kinda," he answered.

I looked to Adam's mother, looking for but not really expecting an explanation.

She chuckled. "I get that face all the time. He was born in Denmark where my husband was raised, but we live in the States now. New York, to be exact. We visit family in Denmark three times a year."

I threw my head back in an, *ooooh, got it*, kind of way. "Wow, that's quite a history you have there." I had risen off the ground, but kept my eyes on Adam and chuckled at the child's confusion of the international affairs within their home.

"And, and, and," Adam continued, motioning to meet him at eye level again. He had a secret to share. "You wanna know what else I'm gonna be?" he asked more excitedly than delivering the news of his role in the Denmark government. The boy squirmed and this time he waited for my guess.

"No, tell me," I shared his glee. Life must have been thrilling for this child, as with all children, I presumed, having nearly everything they came in contact with amaze them.

I encouraged Adam, "Tell me, what else are you going to be when you grow up?"

Adam turned and with raised eyebrows, he asked, "Mommy, can I tell her?"

His mother's face was flushed and rather timidly she replied, "Yes, you can." She sighed and shook her head like a helpless mother.

Adam cupped the side of my face with both his tiny hands and spoke into my ear, forgetting to whisper, "I'm going to be the best big *brothuh* in the *whooole wuhld*." The little boy outstretched his arms and opened his chest to the skies through the ceiling of the airport.

"Wow!" I was taken aback by the squealing in my ear and even more so that I had failed to notice his mother's small protrusion. "Congratulations!" I exclaimed.

"Thank you," she replied, her cheeks blushing. "I'm Seble."

"Hi Seble, I'm Ma'arinet." I smiled. "Are you just coming in from Eritrea, too?"

"We are. We stayed in Denmark for a little while, then in Eritrea for one week, and now we're heading back home. My husband's on a business trip."

"Sweet. What does he do?"

"Jonasi works in commercial development. He's been in his line of work for about four years now." She twirled her hair as she spoke of him, as if he were physically there and she was fighting a schoolgirl crush. It warmed my heart and I found myself clasping my hands on my chest like I was in the middle of a romance movie. "He's a hard worker, I mean sick work ethic, and even still, he's dedicated to his family." She rubbed Adam's hair, but he had grown restless and darted off next to a nearby pillar with his toys.

As Seble spoke of her husband, I thought, *They exist.* I fought the urge to shout a hallelujah. *Good men do, in fact, exist just like I told Sarsum.* Although I believed my words of advice to Sarsum, hearing the testaments of others made me want to jump for joy and scream, *I knew I was right!*

Seble continued to invite me into her life. "I work as a freelance writer. My work schedule is perfect for raising Adam and preparing for little Ia'la here," she caressed a now more visible belly.

Passion flowed from her every word. Seble was a lively woman, one who smiled often and laughed even more. She was humble with her personal accomplishments, and gave just enough of her story to inspire.

Had I not had the giant turn me down, I probably would have made my flight. If I had rushed to the very front of the queue and explained that my flight had just been announced for last boarding call, I would have already been aboard my flight and buckled to my seat. Instead, I let go. And, because of this peace that so strongly made an impression on my mind, I accepted, stayed put, and learned from two perfect strangers.

"That is entirely *too* much time spent on me." Seble pressed her free hand to her cheek, hiding her embarrassment. "What about yourself?" she asked.

I was honored that a woman, one who seemed to have it all, would want to know anything about me. I divulged my story, sharing how it came about that I left for Eritrea and the journey I had traveled before my trip. I even revealed the nightmare I lived in with Esak, but I focused on the end of the relationship and how it opened doors I never even knew existed.

"I freed myself, then ironically, I learned of Eritrea's liberation," I said.

"It was a proud moment in our home, too," Seble shared.

"My parents convinced me to go and I admit, the timing was perfect. I went and God showered me with one blessing after another. I managed to find a woman who led me to my mother's grave. I have never been so fulfilled in my entire life." The more I spoke, the more Seble became visibly emotional. She held one of her hands on her belly, while the other rested on her heart. Seble looked like she was in complete disbelief, almost distraught, so much so that I abruptly stopped speaking.

"What seems to be the matter?" I asked, wondering if I had said something that upset her. "Did I say something?"

"Oh, it's nothing," she answered. "It's just that you remind me so much—"

Attention passengers, this is the final boarding call for Flight 1116 to Chicago. All ticketed passengers should proceed to the gate immediately. Standby passengers should approach the counter for seat assignments. Thank you.

We were halfway through the line when my flight was announced. Adam played on the floor close to the airport security ahead. The booming announcement made it difficult to hear the rest of Seble's thought. We smiled awkwardly at one other, and Seble waited for the translation in German to end before she continued.

"What I was trying to say is that you remind me—"

A gust of wind met my back. A man in a gray suit had darted to the front of the queue, nearly colliding with Seble. I was so focused on our conversation, I had not seen him in time to warn Seble or pull her out of the way.

"Are you okay?" I asked Seble who was more concerned with Adam being trampled at the checkpoint where the man was headed.

He had managed to alarm everyone in the queue, including Adam, who ran over to Seble leaving his toys behind in the chaos and hugged her hips for dear life. It probably was not the smartest thing to do, run up to a security guard at an international airport, but he clearly was a man who needed their assistance. I heard his shouts, but was unable to make out his words. *Whatever the reason for the commotion, it's more than likely not good.*

One nod from the security officer and the man hurled his shiny black shoes into the bins for x-ray review, hastily throwing off his suit jacket. He unbuckled his belt, and flew through the detector.

He must be trying to catch his flight. How amazing it is to let go, to not panic, to be at ease.

Seble and I chuckled at all the interruptions. "You were saying?" I asked as we laughed at the commotion around us.

"I was saying," Seble finished her thought, "that you remind me so much of me."

"How so?" I asked, intrigued by the comparison and careful not to sound too needy for validation or encouragement.

"My past was the greatest resistance to my future, but only because I allowed the pain to remain in my life until the day when I was ready to let it all go. It was like we, my ex-husband and I, were standing on two ends of a depressing game of tug of war," Seble recalled her struggle. "He pulled his end of the rope so incredibly hard and for years I tried to pull my weight and some of his to regain any chance for balance. There were few times when he pulled so hard, it made me fall flat on my face. One day, I woke up, stood up, and I surrendered—not to him, but to God. When I released my hold, he fell back and I sprung forward. I would not be the woman I am today and have the most amazing husband and child if that experience had not occurred in my life. At the end of it all, it forced me to reevaluate my worth, and taught me that *no one* can *ever* rob me of my happiness again."

Seble spoke fondly of a higher power bringing her from darkness and into a guiding light that rewarded her with days of happiness and love, of opportunities and blessings, since the day she decided to live happily.

"With the grace of God and support from a phenomenal family, I came a long way and accomplished more than I had ever dreamed possible," Seble shared.

Chance meetings like this were far from *chance*. I wondered if God laughed when His children uttered the words *chance*, *luck*, *randomness*, and a word I used much too often, *coincidence*.

We reached the security checkpoint and grew more fond of the company we were fortunate enough to have during the otherwise uninteresting act of waiting in line, thanks to Adam's pitcher hands and his toy cowboy.

Good afternoon passengers. This is the pre-boarding announcement for flight 211 to New York City. We are now inviting...

"Place your belongings on the belt and enter through the screen to your right."

I helped Seble with her belongings. Adam struggled to take his colorful backpack off of his own shoulders until I came to his rescue. We soon reached the end of security, and it was time to part ways.

"Thank you for the company and the help." She offered consolation, "And, keep your spirits high. I'm living proof that things not only get better, they become greater than your imagination could ever dream up."

She understands, my thoughts echoed.

We hugged for an extended minute.

Seble hurriedly grabbed for her agenda. She tore a small piece of blank paper and scribbled her contact information. She folded the piece of paper and handed it to me.

"I'll be expecting your call. You're more than welcome to stay with us if you ever want to visit New York."

Seble waved goodbye and I waved back, holding onto the piece of paper. Moments like these were irreplaceable. The Universe had brought this family into my life for a solid reason, I was certain of it. Seble was a snapshot of my future, I firmly believed, and I was able to offer her a glimpse of her own past. I benefited tremendously from an unexpected meeting in a security checkpoint line, and I guessed she did, too.

I opened the piece of paper and took pleasure in the signature below her contact information.

Here for you.
—Seble

Who would have thought?
I fought the urge to skip to my gate.

***

I settled in my window seat, grateful for the gate agent's assistance in booking me on a new flight home.

"Excuse me?"

I had been sitting there for several minutes when I felt a tapping on my right shoulder, interrupting my imagination in all of its fierceness as I slipped further between the graceful lines of a great Brazilian author, Paulo Coelho.

"Yes?" I assumed it was the red-headed male flight attendant requesting my verbal agreement to be in the exit row of the aircraft. My response was curt and came before having even looked up from my novel. When I turned my attention to the voice and caught the gaze of the most handsome man to walk the face of the Earth, dressed in a crisp heather gray suit leaning over the aisle seat in my row, embarrassment took a clout to my cheeks, bruising them immediately.

His skin was the smoothest I had ever seen on a man, apart from facial hair that formed a perfectly shaped, dark goatee. He was sandwiched between the passengers behind and ahead of him. They waited for the front of the line to find their seats, although he seemed perfectly content right where he stood.

"Sorry for interrupting you, but mind keeping me company while I'm stuck here?" he asked. The man who nearly trampled Seble while in the queue was not only staring me in the face, he was speaking to me. And, he was charming.

I looked next to me at two empty seats, then through the space between the headrests behind me. He laughed as I playfully pointed to myself and mouthed, *Me?*

"Oh, so we've got a jokester here." His smile was perfect. "Jeremiah," he announced, outstretching his hand.

"Maari," I replied with a grin as wide as could be, meeting his rough hand with my own. *What could he possibly want with me?*

"I'm actually never this forward, but I was wondering, if that seat next to you is empty when we're in the air, would you mind if I sat there?"

"You're welcome to it, if it's here." I avoided sounding too enthusiastic.

"Great, I'll take you up on that."

An hour later, Jeremiah was tapping on my shoulder again. The two seats had remained empty. Either my neighbors had missed their flights, or the tickets were never sold, or…God was working.

Jeremiah had removed his suit jacket and placed it over his arm. He carried a briefcase on the same side. "You still open to the idea?" He asked, pointing to the middle seat.

I nodded. I was smitten, like it was fifth grade all over again when my first crush, Malcolm, asked to give me my first kiss.

"So, Maari," Jeremiah began. He placed his briefcase in the aisle seat, carefully laying his jacket over it and taking the middle seat for himself. He was a man of integrity, following through with keeping me company. "Do you know what I learned in the last hour?" He sat back in his chair and spoke to the tray in front of him, almost as though he were daydreaming. It reminded me of the questions Reid's wife, Drea, posed.

"No, what?" I asked, melting inside. It was rare for a man this attractive to talk to me, a woman who was broken and trying to build herself up again. I had come a long way, but I had a lot more to go. I rubbed my mother's pendant for comfort, and it immediately put me at ease.

"I learned that the Universe does not, in fact, hate me. I missed my original flight and what I just said about the Universe is what I believed for a split second until I turned my thinking around. I'm glad I did because there's a reason I missed my flight."

To anyone else, he would have sounded like a lunatic, but to me, his words could not have been any clearer a sign.

Jeremiah pointed to the boy and sheep on the cover of my book and said, "I'm sure you know exactly what it is I'm referring to." He paused to see if he was understood.

"I do, I actually do," I replied.

"Where are you from?" he asked, this time facing me. It seemed as though I had his full attention.

"Chicago, and yourself?"

"Great city! I'm from Detroit," Jeremiah replied.

"What brings you to Germany all the way from Detroit?"

"I was in Eritrea working on a coal mining project and visiting family. It was my first trip and I was able to go with my company —translate and help with the strategic planning of extractions and a few other things."

"Very nice." He was a go-getter. *One point*, I thought.

"They tried to keep me out there longer, but I just couldn't do it. I missed my family too much. I haven't seen my parents in over a month. I thought I'd go nuts not seeing my precious mother's face a day longer." Jeremiah was a family man. *One more point*, I thought.

"I know how you feel. I missed my parents, too. I was in Eritrea for two months, and it started to really sting toward the end."

"What were you there for?" Jeremiah asked.

"Visiting family," I answered. I played with my necklace again, and looked away at my dinner tray for a second.

The stewardess interrupted our conversation.

"Chicken or fish?" she asked Jeremiah.

"Chicken," he replied.

"Same for me," I added before she asked.

We brought down our tray tables, and Jeremiah extended his hand, before touching his food. "Do you mind if we pray?"

I would but I need this hand to pinch myself. I placed my hand in his as Jeremiah prayed over our meal. *One hundred extra bonus points please!* I yelled in a silent victory. Although I thought it, I refrained from the Holy Ghost tap dance with my feet.

Natsa may have been onto something, after all. Butterflies swarmed in my stomach, and no one could have paid me to do away with the silly grin on my face.

The first few hours in the clouds were of nonstop conversation, pertaining to everything beneath the sun. I sat in my seat, stunned —first Natsa, then Seble and Adam, and now *him*—Jeremiah. *There's a whole lot of conspiring under the wings of those above,* I thought as Jeremiah spoke of his family with complete adoration, showing me pictures of his siblings and parents. He respected and cherished his family as I wholeheartedly did mine.

In the middle of our conversation, Jeremiah asked, "Maari, if you don't mind, I'd love to see you sometime. Detroit is only a few hours away from Chicago. Would you mind if we exchanged phone numbers?"

"I thought you'd never ask." I dared to be bold. I dared to be forward.

I was reaping the benefits cast by those who watched over me. The whole world seemed to mimic the peace singing in my heart. I nodded in agreement with my destined flight companion. As we prepared for landing, my heart refused to follow, accepting its fate, high among the clouds.

***

I met the outside world with open arms. The wind blew wildly, reminding me there was no other city that felt like my hometown. I handed my two human size suitcases to the cab driver outside of baggage claim and eagerly hopped into the Lebanese man's yellow cab. I had to stop from helping myself to the front passenger seat as I had been accustomed to in Eritrea.

"7407 S. King Drive, please?"

"My pleasure, ma'am." The driver was shorter than me, but lugged my heavy suitcases around like they weighed less than a five-pound dumbbell.

"Where are you coming from?"

"Eritrea!" I realized how awkward my excitement may have been.

"Oh, Ere-tree-ya. I heard about that place on the news. Africa, right?"

"Yes, exactly."

"You guys got free from Ethiopia, I remember."

"That's exactly right!" I was thrilled. A stranger knew of Eritrea.

"Yeah, yeah, Ere-tree-ya. How is it there? Is it nice?"

"It's beautiful."

"Peace make it more beautiful," he added.

"That is very true."

"Your English good. You born here?" He pointed to the floor of the car.

"No, I was born in Eritrea. I came here when I was a little girl."

I smiled at the tingling that met my heart. Independence changed how I presented my motherland. I now could shamelessly claim my country *and* show people that it did in fact exist—and there was a squiggly line to prove it.

I sat silently for the duration of the ride home. I was without my camera and journal, both stowed away in my suitcases. I was left to my thoughts, again.

I can't wait to see mom and dad and share all that I've learned and caught on film! They're going to be so proud of me. I wonder if I should mention Jeremiah. Sarsum would think I was crazy and say it's too soon to know, but my heart doesn't believe that. When I've got a nine-year-old child telling me he's coming, then Seble reflecting on her marriage with Jonasi after her divorce, followed by Jeremiah and I both missing our flights, only to be put on the same one—how could I ignore the signs?

Sarsum…I've missed that voice. Maybe we could plan a trip to Eritrea together. She'd die at how different it is and less judgmental than here. She'd love Aunt Kibra's take on weight!

I've got to show Reid and Drea the pictures of the elderly couple! I wonder how Drea's been feeling. I've got to visit them. Before I left, Reid was still talking about his art studio. I wonder if he's made moves with it.

Art…I am so blessed to be able to do what I love. It's funny but I think my camera lens is my hero, focusing on all that is good. It's the only object I know of that can bring a warm smile to my soul.

As we approached a traffic stop light, an artist on a ladder caught my attention across a busy intersection. In broad daylight, a live graffiti production was in the works. The boy stood tall and steadily on the highest rung of the stepping tool and claimed stake on the bottom of a white billboard. His words were in cursive, almost like the second grade homework assignments that sampled how to write against dashed lines. The graffiti artist had just completed his last letter, the letter *Y*. It was a message meant for me to see.

The phrase, written in a loud heavenly blue, read, "Be Happy."

My heart fluttered, sending a rush of warmth throughout my entire body.

"And, never, ever, let anyone or anything get in your way," I whispered. *If that's not a sign*, I thought as we rode closer to home, *then I don't know what is.*

Epilogue

A letter from Timneet

November 15, 1970

    Adey, I have prayed for you every day since my departure. I have prayed to the stars that they shine over you, that the good Lord deliver a peace that you deserve. Please do not be alarmed by this letter. Aside from how much I miss you and your sweet face, I am well. I wish I had been there to comfort you, to hold and help you. I know in my heart you understand why escaping was the only option I had. It was the hardest decision for me, mainly because of you.

    I have good news to share with you. I am here in Unah. I am but a few days away from being in your presence. You must meet me at Girmai's home. The child that brings you this letter, Sophia, will show you the way. When we meet, please do not fear my size, as this is the other piece of news I have for you. I am carrying your great-grandchild. The father is a boy I met in school, Ne'Amin.

    Adey, I know I will see you soon and we will have time to speak about this all, but these thoughts I would like to share have weighed heavy on my mind and writing them gives me peace. In my heart, I believe I am carrying a girl. I want you to take good care of her when

I return to the battlefield. It pains me that I won't be there to raise her, but when freedom is ours, I will be by her side always. Until then, please make her strong for me. Tell her that I love her. Tell her about me, please. Give her strength from the moment she starts walking. Let her know that whatever trials come her way, I may not physically be there to hear her pain, but I will always have her in my heart.

I cannot wait to see you, Adey. May time speed to bring me near you again. May our love ease the pain of the past.

Until Sunday, Timneet